collected
early
poems of
EZRA
POUND

Ezra Pound in 1909
(Photograph by Elliott and Fry, courtesy of Mrs. Donald Wing)

collected early poems of
EZRA POUND

Edited by Michael John King,
with an introduction by
Louis L. Martz

A NEW DIRECTIONS BOOK

ACKNOWLEDGMENTS
All quotations from the unpublished works of Ezra Pound are given by permission of
The Trustees of the Ezra Pound Literary Property trust; quotations from material in
the Ezra Pound Archive by permission of Yale University Library; "From Chebar" by
permission of the Harriet Monroe Collection, University of Chicago; poems from
proofs of *Canzoni* by permission of the Humanities Research Center, University of
Texas at Austin; quotations from "Hilda's Book" by permission of the Houghton
Library, Harvard University.

"Envoi: *A mon bien aimé*," "From Chebar," "To Hulme (T. E.) and Fitzgerald
(A Certain)," and the fragment "Thoughts moving / in her eyes" were all published
for the first time, in 1976, in *Atlantic Monthly*.

Manufactured in the United States of America
First published clothbound in 1976 and as New Directions Paperbook 540 in 1982
Published simultaneously in Canada by George J. McLeod, Ltd., Toronto

Library of Congress Cataloging in Publication Data

Pound, Ezra, 1885–1972.
    Collected early poems of Ezra Pound.
    (A New Directions Book)
    Includes indexes.
    1. King, Michael John.   II. Title.
[PZ3531.082A17   1982]   811'.52   82-8156
ISBN 0-8112-0843-5 (pbk.)   AACR2

New Directions Books are published for James Laughlin
by New Directions Publishing Corporation,
80 Eighth Avenue, New York 10011

CONTENTS

INTRODUCTION

> And Malrin beheld the broidery of the stars become as
> wind-worn tapestries of ancient wars. And the memory of all
> old songs swept by him as an host blue-robèd trailing in
> dream, Odysseus, and Tristram, and the pale great gods of
> storm, the mailed Campeador and Roland and Villon's
> women and they of Valhalla; as a cascade of dull sapphires
> so poured they out of the mist and were gone.
>
> ("Malrin," p. 33)

We present here a volume that contains ninety-nine poems that Pound
published in his early books but rejected when he made his definitive
selection for *Personae* ("Collected Poems") of 1926; and we also include
twenty-five poems that appeared only in periodicals or miscellanies, along
with thirty-eight previously unpublished poems selected from more than
a hundred unpublished early poems known to exist at Yale, Harvard,
Texas, Chicago, and perhaps other places as well. What is the effect, one
may ask, what is the use, of thus resurrecting so many poems that the
author himself called "a collection of stale creampuffs," when some of
them were republished in 1965? But then he added, with a wry gesture
of affection, echoing his poem "Piccadilly": "Chocolate creams, who hath
forgotten you?"

One might attempt to describe the experience of reading all these
poems by such phrases as "filling the void," "shattering the mist," "banish-
ing the twilight," or, best of all, "escaping from Swinburne to Cathay." For
the first impression one may have from the earliest of these poems has
been rightly set forth by T. S. Eliot in his estimate of the poetical situa-
tion faced by Pound in the first decade of this century: "The question
was still," says Eliot, "where do we go from Swinburne? and the answer
appeared to be, nowhere." [1] It was a problem clearly grasped by Pound
himself in a poem here first published, entitled "Swinburne: A Critique"
(p. 261)—a poem in which Pound, perhaps deliberately, twice spells the
name "Swinbourne," as though he were describing some country from
whose bourne no traveler returns:

> Blazes of color intermingled,
> Wondrous pattern leading nowhere,
> Music without a name,
> Knights that ride in a dream,
> Blind as all men are blind,
> Why should the music show
>   Whither they go?
> I am Swinburne, ruler in mystery.
>   None know the ending,
>   Blazes a-blending   in splendor

Of glory none know the meaning on,
I am he that paints the rainbow of the sunset
And the end of all dreams,
                    Wherefor would ye know?
                    Honor the glow
Of the colors   care not wherefore   they gleam
                    All things but seem.

It is a brilliant evocation of Swinburne-land, as Pound himself fre-
quently created it in his own early poems—a land of dreams and sorrows
derived not simply from Swinburne, but also from Rossetti and the other
Pre-Raphaelites with whom Swinburne began his career; and also from
the heirs of Swinburne, the "Decadent" poets of the 'Nineties, Dowson,
Davidson, Lionel Johnson, and the rest, especially the early Yeats, with
his Celtic variations on the Swinburnian dream. These are poems, in
Pound's own phrase, "That Pass between the False Dawn and the True"—
the title of a discarded poem (p. 29):

Blown of the winds whose goal is "No-man-knows"
As feathered seeds upon the wind are borne,
To kiss as winds kiss and to melt as snows
And in our passing taste of all men's scorn,
Wraiths of a dream that fragrant ever blows
From out the night we know not to the morn,
Borne upon winds whose goal is "No-man-knows."

But even as he mastered this melancholy, languid manner of writing,
Pound was reaching far beyond the 'Nineties, as in another poem here
first published, "The Summons" (p. 262), addressed to a lady who seems
to be an image of poetic inspiration (perhaps, literally, "H.D."):

I cannot bow to woo thee
With honey words and flower kisses
And the dew of sweet half-truths
Fallen on the grass of old quaint love-tales
Of broidered days foredone.
Nor in the murmurous twilight
May I sit below thee,
Worshiping in whispers
Tremulous as far-heard bells.

All this faded idiom, he says, "is gone/ As the shadow of the wind." The
echo of Dowson's most famous phrase shows the immediate ancestry of
the foregoing lines, but not of the following Dantesque vision:

But as I am ever swept upward
To the centre of all truth
So must I bear thee with me
Rapt into this great involving flame,
Calling ever from the midst thereof,
    "Follow! Follow!"
And in the glory of our meeting
Shall the power be reborn.

Pound knew that the power of the masters, Rossetti and Swinburne, had been diluted and enervated by the languid eroticism, the misty land-scapes, the melancholy dreams, and the pallid archaisms of their followers, and while the mode attracted him, he knew it had no future. Thus he could imitate the "Celtic Twilight" of Yeats in "La Fraisne" (and indeed he planned to make "La Fraisne" the title-poem of his first volume), but he could also ridicule "the impassioned rehash of the mystically beautiful celtic mythology" in his ballad of "P'ti'cru" (p. 273), though, like his "Critique" of Swinburne, the ballad remained unpublished. Thus too in "The Decadence" (p. 44) we find admiration for those poets' devotion to the cause of Art, along with an undertone that seems to mock their self-pity and their posture of exhausted heroism:

Tarnished we! Tarnished! Wastrels all!
And yet the art goes on, goes on.
Broken our strength, yea as crushed reeds we fall,
And yet the art, the *art* goes on. . . .

Broken our manhood for the wrack and strain;
Drink of our hearts the sunset and the cry
"Io Triumphe!" Tho our lips be slain
We see Art vivant, and exult to die.

Pound knew that somehow he must discover a source of imaginative power such as Swinburne himself had found in the Greeks, as Pound shows in his perfervid tribute to Swinburne, written three years before Swinburne's death in 1909, and appropriately published in Pound's first volume, 1908. It bears the title "Salve O Pontifex!" with the subtitle "To Swinburne; an hemichaunt" (p. 40). The last phrase sums up the heavily mannered archaism of the 'Nineties in which this tribute and most of Pound's earliest poems abound:

One after one do they leave thee,
    High Priest of Iacchus,
Toning thy melodies even as winds tone
The whisper of tree leaves, on sun-lit days . . .

(Iacchus being the deity of the Eleusinian mysteries and a deity assimilated to Bacchus, perhaps through the similarity of name.)

Wherefor tho thy co-novices bent to the scythe
Of the magian wind that is voice of Prosephone,
Leaving thee solitary, master of initiating
Maenads that come thru the
Vine-entangled ways of the forest
Seeking, out of all the world
        Madness of Iacchus,
That being skilled in the secrets of the double cup
They might turn the dead of the world
Into beauteous paeans,
        O High Priest of Iacchus . . .
            Breathe!
Now that evening cometh upon thee,
Breathe upon us that low-bowed and exultant
Drink wine of Iacchus . . .
        O High Priest of Iacchus
Breathe thou upon us
        Thy magic in parting!

"Balderdash," Pound added in a note when he reprinted the poem in 1917—"but let it stand for the rhythm," he apologized. Clearly, even as late as that, the spell of Swinburne was upon him, and indeed it never wholly left him, for even in the prison camp at Pisa the Greek gods of Swinburne are present in the great lynx-hymn of Canto 79, with its cries of "Iacchos," "Iacche." What he admired in Swinburne was more than the rhythm. It was Swinburne's power to evoke the gods of the past and thus compensate in some measure for the mercantile and industrial world of Victoria from which the gods had departed in despair, leaving behind the gray world of Matthew Arnold's woman who has forsaken her beloved Merman:

She steals to the window, and looks at the sand;
And over the sand at the sea;
And her eyes are set in a stare;
And anon there breaks a sigh,
And anon there drops a tear,
From a sorrow-clouded eye,
And a heart sorrow-laden,
A long, long sigh,
For the cold strange eyes of a little Mermaiden,
And the gleam of her golden hair.

This is the sort of thing that drew from Pound's friend T. E. Hulme his violent objection to the weeping ruins of romanticism: "I object," says Hulme, "to the sloppiness which doesn't consider that a poem is a poem unless it is moaning or whining about something or other . . . The thing has got so bad now that a poem which is all dry and hard, a properly classical poem, would not be considered poetry at all . . . Poetry that isn't damp isn't poetry at all . . . There is a general tendency to think that verse means little else than the expression of unsatisfied emotion." Hulme then went on to recommend his famous antidotes to all this dampness: "It is essential to prove that beauty may be in small, dry things . . . The great aim is accurate, precise and definite description . . . the particular verse we are going to get will be cheerful, dry and sophisticated." [2]

Such were the views that Hulme and Pound came to share after their first meeting in 1909, and so it is no wonder that, in 1911, Pound should publish his "Song in the Manner of Housman" (p. 163):

> O woe, woe
> People are born and die,
> We also shall be dead pretty soon
> Therefore let us act as if we were
> dead already.

> The bird sits on the hawthorn tree
> But he dies also, presently.
> Some lads get hung, and some get shot.
> Woeful is this human lot.
> *Woe! woe, etcetera. . . .*

But Pound's dissatisfaction with this dampness had been manifested earlier, in a poem published near the end of *Personae* (1909): "Revolt: Against the Crepuscular Spirit in Modern Poetry" (p. 96)—a poem that denounces and renounces the mode of many of the poems that precede it in this book:

> I would shake off the lethargy of this our time,
> and give
> For shadows—shapes of power
> For dreams—men.

> "It is better to dream than do"?
> Aye! and, No!

> Aye! if we dream great deeds, strong men,
> Hearts hot, thoughts mighty.

> No! if we dream pale flowers,
> Slow-moving pageantry of hours that languidly
> Drop as o'er-ripened fruit from sallow trees . . .

> Great God, if men are grown but pale sick phantoms
> That must live only in these mists and tempered lights
> And tremble for dim hours that knock o'er loud
> Or tread too violent in passing them;

Great God, if these thy sons are grown such thin ephemera,
I bid thee grapple chaos and beget
Some new titanic spawn to pile the hills and stir
This earth again.

But where will the voices be found to scatter the shadows and stir the earth? In Robert Browning, certainly, whose strident voice is humorously imitated in "Mesmerism" (p. 17), and whose bracing impact upon the whole Victorian scene Pound represents in a poem to Elizabeth Barrett Browning, here first published (p. 262). The voice of Browning is clear in many of these early monologues, in "Cino," "Marvoil," "Piere Vidal Old," in the long poem here first published, "Capilupus Sends Greeting to Grotus," and in many other places, as late as the bitter parody in Canto 80: "Oh to be in England now that Winston's out." But the impact of Browning is far from dominant in these early poems, far less significant than it appears in the *Personae* of 1926, where Pound retains nine of his most Browningesque poems, while discarding more than sixty that tell of crepuscular times.

The masks that Pound adopts usually derive from other promptings: from Yeats, from Ovid ("An Idyl for Glaucus"), from Rossetti, and from the literally pre-raphaelite poets that Rossetti revived in his great translations of Dante, Cavalcanti, and the other medieval Tuscan poets. Introducing his own versions of Cavalcanti, published in 1912, Pound says: "In the matter of these translations and of my knowledge of Tuscan poetry, Rossetti is my mother and my father." Pound read all these poets in the Temple Classics edition, where Rossetti's translations were reprinted; Pound's own volumes still exist, heavily annotated. Then there was the Villon that Swinburne praised and translated, and Pound's own discoveries, the medieval troubadours of Provence or the Anglo-Saxon poet of "The Seafarer."

Deeper still, Pound's varied ways of speaking in dramatic monologue seem to be based upon his sense of a prophetic mission, *prophetic* in the basic Greek sense. For a prophet, in Greek, is first of all "one who speaks for another." This may mean "one who interprets the will of a god," or one who speaks through some divine inspiration; thus poets were called prophets (interpreters) of the Muses, and more generally, the word prophet might be applied to an interpreter of scripture or to an inspired teacher. ("I do not teach—I awake," says Pound in a manuscript note to "Histrion.") Pound also takes on the role of a Biblical prophet, as in the manuscript poem of 1913 entitled "From Chebar" (p. 269)—the reference being to the first verse of Ezekiel: "In the thirtieth year, in the fourth month, on the fifth day of the month, as I was among the exiles by the river Chebar, the heavens were opened, and I saw visions of God." It is a poem that mingles a Biblical rhythm with the prophetic strain of Walt Whitman:

Before you were, America!

I did not begin with you,
I do not end with you, America. . . .

Oh I can see you,
I with the maps to aid me,
I can see the coast and the forest
And the corn-yellow plains and the hills,
The domed sky and the jagged,
The plainsmen and men of the cities. . . .

I have seen the dawn mist
Move in the yellow grain,
I have seen the daubed purple sunset;
You may kill me, but I do not accede,
You may ignore me, you may keep me in exile,
You may assail me with negations, or you
          may keep me, a while, well hidden,
But I am after you and before you,
And above all, I do not accede. . . .

"There is no use your quoting Whitman against me," he adds, even as he writes in Whitman's cadence: "His time is not our time, his day and hour were different." The whole poem derives from Pound's profound conviction that the arts constitute a moral, civilizing instrument:

The order does not end in the arts,
The order shall come and pass through them.

The state is too idle, the decrepit church is too idle,
The arts alone can transmit this.
They alone cling fast to the gods . . .

That is one role of the prophet—a role that grew upon Pound as he grew older, but it is related to the earlier prophetic role that he describes in the discarded poem (p. 71) "Histrion" ("Actor"):

No man hath dared to write this thing as yet,
And yet I know, how that the souls of all men great
At times pass through us,
And we are melted into them, and are not
Save reflexions of their souls.
Thus am I Dante for a space and am
One François Villon, ballad-lord and thief
Or am such holy ones I may not write,
Lest blasphemy be writ against my name;
This for an instant and the flame is gone.

'Tis as in midmost us there glows a sphere
Translucent, molten gold, that is the "I"
And into this some form projects itself:
Christus, or John, or eke the Florentine;
And as the clear space is not if a form's
Imposed thereon,
So cease we from all being for the time,
And these, the Masters of the Soul, live on.

What Pound seems to be describing here (beneath the histrionic clap-trap) is his own sense of his remarkable mimetic genius, his ability to absorb the style, manner, and meaning of another poet, and then to interpret and recreate that role, in translation, in creative adaptation, or in original poems in a particular kind of writing. His masks, his personae, are modes of poetry: masks through which the modern poet transmits his apprehension of the past and makes it available to the present, as a civilizing force. This is truly to be a prophet of the Muses. Hence the motto that concludes *A Lume Spento* (1908) and begins *Personae* (1909): "Make-strong old dreams lest this our world lose heart."

All this is related to Pound's belief in a principle that runs throughout his early poetry and underlies the Cantos: the belief that the poetic power breaks through the crust of daily life and apprehends a transcendent flow of spirit, or energy, or divine power, which Pound calls "the gods." His poetic imagination attempts to live in an animate universe, where things of nature and beyond nature can be merged with inner man, as he explains in a note in the San Trovaso Notebook:

> All art begins in the physical discontent (or torture) of loneliness and partiality [i.e. being only a separate part of existence].
>
> It is to fill this lack that man first spun shapes out of the void. And with the intensity of this longing gradually came unto him power, power over the essences of the dawn, over the filaments of light and the warp of melody . . .
>
> Of such perceptions rise the ancient myths of the origin of demi-gods. Even as the ancient myths of metamorphosis rise out of flashes of cosmic consciousness.

Thus, as he seems to say in the discarded poem "Plotinus" (p. 36), such perceptions grow from within man and reach outward toward the eternal.

This is what happens in his many poems of love for woman, where he adopts the image of an ideal woman as his inspiration, after the manner of Dante and Cavalcanti and the troubadours of Provence. An apt example of how these readings in the medieval poets showed him a way of escaping from the Swinburnian twilight is found in the curious history of the poem which appeared in 1908 under the title "Vana"—"empty things," "fruitless things." But the title holds a certain irony, for the "vain" thing in the end proves to be the effort to deny the creative desire for "song": the magical, fertile words are within the lonely speaker, crying for a song that has not yet been created:

> In vain have I striven
>   to teach my heart to bow;
> In vain have I said to him
>   "There be many singers   greater than thou."

But his answer cometh,   as winds and as lutany,
As a vague crying upon the night
That leaveth me no rest,   saying ever,
         "Song,   a song."

        Their echoes play upon each other in the twilight
        Seeking ever a song.
        Lo, I am worn with travail
        And the wandering of many roads hath made my eyes
        As dark red circles filled with dust.
        Yet there is a trembling upon me in the twilight,
                And little red elf words   crying "A song,"
                Little grey elf words   crying for a song,
                Little brown leaf words   crying "A song,"
                Little green leaf words   crying for a song.
        The words are as leaves, old brown leaves in the spring time
        Blowing they know not whither, seeking a song.

That is a perfect expression of the twilight of the 'Nineties, the poetic imagination seeking expression, but finding no voice, no poetical way out of the gloom. Then in 1909 the poem reappears in *Personae* under the title "Praise of Ysolt"—but here it forms the first twenty lines of a poem that runs to fifty-eight lines. Whether the first part was written separately or whether this was all written as one piece and only the first part published in 1908, we do not know; in any case the important point is that the sequel of 1909 tells how the speaker's *soul* (seat of the intellect), as distinguished from his *heart* (seat of the feelings), has escaped from its empty state by responding, like Dante, to the memory of a woman of transcendent power:

        But my soul sent a woman, a woman of the wonderfolk,
        A woman as fire upon the pine woods
                crying "Song, a song."
        As the flame crieth unto the sap.
        My song was ablaze with her and she went from me
        As flame leaveth the embers so went she unto new
                forests
        And the words were with me
                crying ever "Song, a song."

        And I "I have no song,"
        Till my soul sent a woman as the sun:
        Yea as the sun calleth to the seed,
        As the spring upon the bough
        So is she that cometh the song-drawer
        She that holdeth the wonder words within her eyes . . .

In poems such as these one has the sense of a tormented, lonely genius crying for release from a faded idiom, seeking a way in which his song can emerge into a sort of naked clarity, free of archaic diction and dead poetical properties. Even in these early days, his natural manner of writing seems to have been much simpler and more direct than his published manner, as the manuscript version of "Idyl for Glaucus" seems to suggest (see textual notes); but the idiom of the 'Nineties called for the imposition of stilted inversions and archaisms. Nevertheless Pound is everywhere seeking a song that he can call his own, and here and there, perfectly, he finds it, as in "Francesca" (p. 121), where the Dantesque name presides over a poem of our own immediate world and language:

> You came in out of the night
> And there were flowers in your hands,
> Now you will come out of a confusion of people,
> Out of a turmoil of speech about you.
>
> I who have seen you amid the primal things
> Was angry when they spoke your name
> In ordinary places.
> I would that the cool waves might flow over
>   my mind,
> And that the world should dry as a dead leaf,
> Or as a dandelion seed-pod and be swept away,
> So that I might find you again,
> Alone.

There is the free verse, the supple language, the clear imagery that marks most of the poems in *Ripostes* (1912), but it is a poem published in 1909.

Everywhere, throughout these early volumes, one feels the unsteady oscillation between the dream world of the Swinburnians and another world in which moments of human experience are caught in a modern language and a modern movement. Thus in *Exultations* (1909), only two pages before "Francesca," we come upon the discarded sequence "Laudantes Decem Pulchritudinis Johannae Templi" (p. 117). Mary de Rachewiltz has suggested a convincing explanation of that enigmatic title: "Joan of the Temple" is the Giovanna ("Joan" in Rossetti's version) of Dante's *Vita Nuova* and Cavalcanti's sonnets—which Pound read in the Temple edition, making especially heavy annotations upon Cavalcanti's sonnets to this lady. It is a characteristic Poundian twist, with the Tuscan lady (also called "Primavera") working within a predominantly Yeatsian sequence: "When your beauty is grown old in all men's songs . . . O Rose of the sharpest thorn! / O Rose of the crimson beauty . . . The unappeasable loveliness / is calling to me out of the wind . . ." And then, with a typical Yeatsian subheading:

He speaks to the moonlight concerning the Beloved.
Pale hair that the moon has shaken
Down over the dark breast of the sea,
O magic her beauty has shaken
About the heart of me;
Out of you have I woven a dream
That shall walk in the lonely vale
Betwixt the high hill and the low hill;
Until the pale stream
Of the souls of men quench and grow still.

Yet in the midst of all this tapestry of echoes, one comes upon the eighth section with surprise, for here, suddenly, the rose imagery is drawn into the mind of the speaker, who ponders the problem of memory in a delicate and subtle way, as the movements of the verse mirror the hesitations and nuances of the mind in action:

If the rose-petals which have fallen upon my eyes
And if the perfect faces which I see at times
When my eyes are closed—
Faces fragile, pale, yet flushed a little, like petals
        of roses:
If these things have confused my memories of her
So that I could not draw her face
Even if I had skill and the colours,
Yet because her face is so like these things
They but draw me nearer unto her in my thought
And thoughts of her come upon my mind gently,
As dew upon the petals of roses.

This is no dream: the motion of thought re-enacts the effort of memory so often represented in Dante or Cavalcanti: *dove sta memoria*. Here is verse with an intellectual base, a rational element working its way out of the dream and the lethargy and the twilight of depleted feelings.

In another partly discarded sequence, "Und Drang" (p. 167), the twelve poems concluding *Canzoni* (1911) move through a series of masks that seem to reflect the various aspects of Pound's early poetical experience. The opening voice here seems to be that of a lost follower of Nietzsche:

I am worn faint,
The winds of good and evil
Blind me with dust
And burn me with the cold,
There is no comfort being over-man;
Yet are we come more near
The great oblivions and the labouring night,
Inchoate truth and the sepulchral forces.

The poem then moves through memories of bitterness and pain, changing from belief to a state where "The will to live goes from me," and from there to a Yeatsian memory when "I was Aengus for a thousand years." Section IV is an elegy for the Decadents, a recreation of their sombre hedonism:

> All things in season and no thing o'er long!
> Love and desire and gain and good forgetting,
> Thou canst not stay the wheel, hold none too long!

In section V the voice of a critical commentator enters, clearing away the crépuscule:

> How our modernity,
> Nerve-wracked and broken, turns
> Against time's way and all the way of things,
> Crying with weak and egoistic cries!

This speaker knows that "the restless will / Surges amid the stars / Seeking new moods of life, / New permutations." And soon the new moods come. Section VI brings us into a theater where, between the acts, the speaker catches a glimpse of a beloved face in something very close to the kind of intense moment exalted by Walter Pater:

> A little light,
> The gold, and half the profile!
> The whole face
> Was nothing like you, yet that image cut
> Sheer through the moment.

He goes on seeking the face "in the flurry of Fifth Avenue," and then in Section VII we emerge into "The House of Splendour," a perfect poem in its kind—a vision out of Cavalcanti and his peers, through Rossetti:

> And I have seen my Lady in the sun,
> Her hair was spread about, a sheaf of wings,
> And red the sunlight was, behind it all.

Section VIII, "The Flame," pursues a transcendent vision through allusions to Provence and "Oisin":

> There *is* the subtler music, the clear light
> Where time burns back about th' eternal embers.
> We are not shut from all the thousand heavens:
> Lo, there are many gods whom we have seen,
> Folk of unearthly fashion, places splendid,
> Bulwarks of beryl and of chrysoprase.

Then, after two four-line "inscriptions" commemorating the past, the poem moves forward into the present, with a language, wit, and attitude that T. E. Hulme must have relished:

> I suppose, when poetry comes down to facts,
> When our souls are returned to the gods
> and the spheres they belong in,
> Here in the every-day where our acts
> Rise up and judge us;
>
> I suppose there are a few dozen verities
> That no shift of mood can shake from us:
>
> One place where we'd rather have tea
> (Thus far hath modernity brought us)
> "Tea" (Damn you!)
> Have tea, damn the Caesars,
> Talk of the latest success, give wing to some scandal,
> Garble a name we detest, and for prejudice?
> Set loose the whole consummate pack
> to bay like Sir Roger de Coverley's.

And the sequence ends, appropriately, with a poem that teases a famous, very fragile poem by Yeats, "The Cap and Bells."

The sequence "Und Drang" deserves to be read entire as a self-conscious version of Pound's efforts to imitate and then to disengage his muse from nineteenth-century trappings and move into his own world. Yet even in *Riposte* (1912) the oscillations are evident, as within the poem "N.Y." (p. 185), where his prophetic voice speaks to the city with love and hope, while the murmur of the realist tells the prophet that his efforts are in vain:

> My City, my beloved, my white! Ah, slender,
> Listen! Listen to me, and I will breathe into thee a soul.
> Delicately upon the reed, attend me!
>
> *Now do I know that I am mad.*
> *For here are a million people surly with traffic;*
> *This is no maid.*
> *Neither could I play upon any reed if I had one.*
>
> My City, my beloved,
> Thou art a maid with no breasts,
> Thou art slender as a silver reed.
> Listen to me, attend me!
> And I will breathe into thee a soul,
> And thou shalt live for ever.

Or we may contrast the Swinburnian sapphics of "Apparuit" (another complex union of Dante and the 'Nineties) with the London salon world of "Portrait d'une Femme." As in "The Needle," Pound's career stands at the turn of a tide. He has beat the 'Nineties at their own game (indeed, except for Yeats, Pound might be called the best poet of the 'Nineties!). He has matched the intricate stanza-forms of Provence or Tuscany in *Canzoni* (1911), has seen the Greek gods making their tentative return (p. 198), has even begun to make his peace with Whitman, as he says in an essay of 1909:

> Mentally I am a Walt Whitman who has learned to wear a collar and a dress shirt (although at times inimical to both). Personally I might be very glad to conceal my relationship to my spiritual father and brag about my more congenial ancestry—Dante, Shakespeare, Theocritus, Villon, but the descent is a bit difficult to establish. And, to be frank, Whitman is to my fatherland . . . what Dante is to Italy and I at my best can only be a strife for a renaissance in America of all the lost or temporarily mislaid beauty, truth, valor, glory of Greece, Italy, England and all the rest of it.[3]

But how does one deliberately start a Renaissance? Pound knew. As he wrote in 1915: "The first step of a renaissance, or awakening, is the importation of models for painting, sculpture or writing . . . We must learn what we can from the past, we must learn what other nations have done successfully under similar circumstances, we must think how they did it." The first step, then, is what he calls the preparation of the "palette": we must find in foreign literature the "pure colors" out of which a new poetry, created by America for all the world, will arise.[4]

Now, in 1912, Pound felt that the palette had been prepared, for in that year Pound sent to Harriet Monroe, for publication in her new magazine, a poem entitled "Epilogue" (p. 209), in which he offered to America his versions and studies of medieval poetry, as spoils brought from Europe to enrich his own beloved country. He could not know that one more "pure color," perhaps the most important of all, remained for him to receive: a pigment indispensable to the development of his poetical future, indispensable to the structure, movement, and meaning of his Cantos. In the very next year the gift arrived, from an unexpected quarter.

In 1913 Ernest Fenollosa's widow, in an act of inspired intuition, saw in Pound the poet who would understand her husband's studies in Chinese poetry and the Japanese drama, and she gave Fenollosa's papers to Pound to work with as he would. In those papers Pound discovered the fulfillment of his deepest poetical needs: another country, another kingdom, as different from Swinburneland as one could ever wish. Here was an ancient, established civilization, preserved in poetry of local realism, touched with sadness, aware of mortality, but never overcome with melancholy. Here was poetry of live, precise detail, mingling a love of nature with a love of man. And best of all, the materials were free for him to recreate within the matrix of his own developed craft. For Fenollosa's notes gave him English equivalents for Chinese characters, but no ancient forms of meter or rime to be followed. The lonely void was suddenly filled with the riches of an entire civilization, ready to be transmitted by his highly prepared and adaptable muse. So *Cathay,* that ideal kingdom, came into being: Pound's first perfect book, or rather booklet, and one that presented Pound's mature voice through a new mask, colloquial in language, precise in imagery, free and flexible in its movement, as in the opening words of *Cathay* ("Song of the Bowmen of Shu"), where the calendar of hardship and sorrow is revealed and controlled by the changing imagery of fern-shoots:

> Here we are, picking the first fern-shoots
> And saying: When shall we get back to our country?
> Here we are because we have the Ken-nin for our foemen,
> We have no comfort because of these Mongols.
> We grub the soft fern-shoots,
> When anyone says "Return," the others are full of sorrow.
> Sorrowful minds, sorrow is strong, we are hungry and thirsty.
> Our defence is not yet made sure, no one can let his friend
>   return.
> We grub the old fern-stalks.

This is hardly the cheerful verse that Hulme foresaw; the coming of war had dashed that hope. But now Pound's experience in working with Chinese poetry enables him to "abbreviate" Hulme's conversation about trench warfare into a powerful poem (p. 286) of accurate, precise, and definite description.

"The last century rediscovered the middle ages," Pound wrote in February 1915, already casting his medieval studies into the past. "It is possible," he added, looking forward, "that this century may find a new Greece in China . . . Undoubtedly pure color is to be found in Chinese poetry, when we begin to know enough about it; indeed, a shadow of this perfection is already at hand in translations." [5] Close at hand—for only two months later, *Cathay* appeared.

Louis L. Martz

NOTES

¹ T. S. Eliot, "Ezra Pound," in *An Examination of Ezra Pound,* ed. Peter Russell (London and New York, 1950), p. 25; London title: *Ezra Pound, A Collection of Essays.* Eliot's essay originally appeared in *Poetry, 68* (1946), 326–38.

² T. E. Hulme, "Romanticism and Classicism," in *Speculations* (London and New York, 1924), pp. 126–27, 131–32, 137.

³ Ezra Pound, *Selected Prose, 1909–1965,* ed. William Cookson (London and New York, 1973), pp. 115–16.

⁴ Ezra Pound, "The Renaissance," in *Literary Essays,* ed. T. S. Eliot (London and New York, 1954), pp. 214–19. The essays under this title, "The Renaissance," originally appeared in *Poetry* for February, March, and May, 1915; the date 1914 in *Literary Essays* is an error.

⁵ *Literary Essays,* pp. 215, 218. Pound's version of Li Po's "Exile's Letter" appeared in *Poetry* for March, 1915; *Cathay* appeared in April, 1915.

The following very helpful studies of Pound's early poetry should be consulted: N. Christoph de Nagy, *The Poetry of Ezra Pound: the Pre-Imagist Stage,* Bern, 1960; and *Ezra Pound's Poetics and Literary Tradition: The Critical Decade,* Bern, 1966; Thomas H. Jackson, *The Early Poetry of Ezra Pound,* Cambridge, Mass., 1968; Herbert N. Schneidau, *Ezra Pound, the Image and the Real,* Baton Rouge, 1969; Hugh Witemeyer, *The Poetry of Ezra Pound: Forms and Renewal, 1908–1920,* Berkeley and Los Angeles, 1969.

A LUME SPENTO

1908

Ezra Pound (signature)

A
LUME
SPENTO

EZRA POUND.

Title page of A Lume Spento *(with Pound's signature and home address)*

Published A. ANTONINI
Cannaregio, 923 - VENICE (Italy)

Lire 5.

IN THE CITY OF ALDUS
MCMVIII.

Verso of title page, A Lume Spento

This Book was

LA FRAISNE

(THE ASH TREE)

dedicated

> *to such as love this same*
> *beauty that I love, somewhat*
> *after mine own fashion.*

But sith one of them has gone out very quickly from amongst us it given

A LUME SPENTO

(WITH TAPERS QUENCHED)

in memoriam eius mihi caritate primus

William Brooke Smith

Painter, Dreamer of dreams.

Dedication, A Lume Spento

GRACE BEFORE SONG

Lord God of heaven that with mercy dight
Th' alternate prayer wheel of the night and light
Eternal hath to thee, and in whose sight
Our days as rain drops in the sea surge fall,

As bright white drops upon a leaden sea
Grant so my songs to this grey folk may be:

As drops that dream and gleam and falling catch the sun,
Evan'scent mirrors every opal one
Of such his splendor as their compass is,
So, bold My Songs, seek ye such death as this.

"When the soul is exhausted of fire, then doth the spirit return unto its primal nature and there is upon it a peace great and of the woodland

"magna pax et silvestris."

Then becometh it kin to the faun and the dryad, a woodland-dweller amid the rocks and streams

"consociis faunis dryadisque inter saxa sylvarum"

Janus of Basel.*

Also has Mr. Yeats in his "Celtic Twilight" treated of such, and I because in such a mood, feeling myself divided between myself corporal and a self aetherial "a dweller by streams and in woodland," eternal because simple in elements

"Aeternus quia simplex naturae"

Being freed of the weight of a soul "capable of salvation or damnation," a grievous striving thing that after much straining was mercifully taken from me; as had one passed saying as one in the Book of the Dead,

"I, lo I, am the assembler of souls," and had taken it with him, leaving me thus *simplex naturae,* even so at peace and trans-sentient as a wood pool I made it.

The Legend thus: "Miraut de Garzelas, after the pains he bore a-loving Riels of Calidorn and that to none avail, ran mad in the forest.

"Yea even as Peire Vidal ran as a wolf for her of Penautier tho some say that twas folly or as Garulf Bisclavret so ran truly, till the King brought him respite (See "Lais" Marie de France), so was he ever by the Ash Tree."

Hear ye his speaking: (low, slowly he speaketh it, as one drawn apart, reflecting) (égaré).

* Referendum for contrast. "Daemonalitas" of the Rev. Father Sinistrari of Ameno (1600 circ). "A treatise wherein is shown that there are in existence on earth rational creatures besides man, endowed like him with a body and soul, that are born and die like him, redeemed by our Lord Jesus-Christ, and capable of receiving salvation or damnation." Latin and English text. pub. Liseux. Paris, 1879.

LA FRAISNE

(Scene: The Ash Wood of Malvern)

For I was a gaunt, grave councilor
Being in all things wise, and very old,
But I have put aside this folly and the cold
That old age weareth for a cloak.

I was quite strong—at least they said so—
The young men at the sword-play;
But I have put aside this folly, being gay
In another fashion that more suiteth me.

I have curled mid the boles of the ash wood,
I have hidden my face where the oak
Spread his leaves over me, and the yoke
Of the old ways of men have I cast aside.

By the still pool of Mar-nan-otha
Have I found me a bride
That was a dog-wood tree some syne.
She hath called me from mine old ways
She hath hushed my rancour of council,
Bidding me praise

Naught but the wind that flutters in the leaves.

She hath drawn me from mine old ways,
Till men say that I am mad;
But I have seen the sorrow of men, and am glad,
For I know that the wailing and bitterness are a folly.

And I? I have put aside all folly and all grief.
I wrapped my tears in an ellum leaf
And left them under a stone
And now men call me mad because I have thrown
All folly from me, putting it aside
To leave the old barren ways of men,
Because my bride

9

Is a pool of the wood and
Tho all men say that I am mad
It is only that I am glad,
Very glad, for my bride hath toward me a great love
That is sweeter than the love of women
That plague and burn and drive one away.

Aie-e! 'Tis true that I am gay
    Quite gay, for I have her alone here
    And no man troubleth us.

Once when I was among the young men . . . .
And they said I was quite strong, among the young men.
Once there was a woman . . . .
. . . . but I forget . . . . she was . . . .
. . . . I hope she will not come again.

. . . . I do not remember . . . .
I think she hurt me once but . . . .
That was very long ago.

I do not like to remember things any more.

I like one little band of winds that blow
In the ash trees here:
For we are quite alone
Here mid the ash trees.

CINO

                    (Italian Campagna 1309, the open road)

"Bah! I have sung women in three cities,
But it is all the same;
And I will sing of the sun.

Lips, words, and you snare them,
Dreams, words, and they are as jewels,

Strange spells of old deity,
Ravens, nights, allurement:
And they are not;
Having become the souls of song.

Eyes, dreams, lips, and the night goes.
Being upon the road once more,
They are not.
Forgetful in their towers of our tuneing
Once for Wind-runeing
They dream us-toward and
Sighing, say "Would Cino,
"Passionate Cino, of the wrinkling eyes,
"Gay Cino, of quick laughter,
"Cino, of the dare, the jibe,
"Frail Cino, strongest of his tribe
"That tramp old ways beneath the sun-light,
"Would Cino of the Luth were here!

Once, twice, a year—
Vaguely thus word they:
        "Cino?" "Oh, eh, Cino Polnesi
        "The singer is't you mean?"
        "Ah yes, passed once our way,
        "A saucy fellow, but . . . .
        "(Oh they are all one these vagabonds),
        "Peste! 'tis his own songs?
        "Or some other's that he sings?
        "But *you,* My Lord, how with your city?"

But you "My Lord," God's pity!
And all I knew were out, My Lord, you
Were Lack-land Cino, e'en as I am
O Sinistro.

I have sung women in three cities.
But it is all one.
I will sing of the sun.
. . . . eh? . . . . they mostly had grey eyes,
But it is all one, I will sing of the sun.

" 'Pollo Phoibee, old tin pan you
Glory to Zeus' aegis-day
Shield o'steel-blue, th' heaven o'er us
Hath for boss thy lustre gay!

'Pollo Phoibee, to our way-fare
Make thy laugh our wander-lied;
Bid thy 'fulgence bear away care.
Cloud and rain-tears pass they fleet!

Seeking e'er the new-laid rast-way
To the gardens of the sun . . . .

. . . .
. . . .

I have sung women in three cities
But it is all one.

I will sing of the white birds
In the blue waters of heaven,
The clouds that are spray to its sea.

IN EPITAPHIUM EIUS

Servant and singer, Troubadour
That for his loving, loved each fair face more
Than craven sluggard can his life's one love,

Dowered with love, "whereby the sun doth move
And all the stars."
They called him fickle that the lambent flame
Caught "Bicé" dreaming in each new-blown name,

And loved all fairness tho its hidden guise
Lurked various in half an hundred eyes;

That loved the essence tho each casement bore
A different semblance than the one before.

NA AUDIART

(Que be-m vols mal)

Note: Any one who has read anything of the troubadours knows well the tale of Bertran of Born and My Lady Maent of Montaignac, and knows also the song he made when she would none of him, the song wherein he, seeking to find or make her equal, begs of each preëminent lady of Langue d'Oc some trait or some fair semblance: thus of Cembelins her "esgart amoros" to wit, her love-lit glance, of Aelis her speech free-running, of the Vicomptess of Chales her throat and her two hands, at Roacoart of Anhes her hair golden as Iseult's; and even in this fashion of Lady Audiart "altho she would that ill come unto him" he sought and praised the lineaments of the torse. And all this to make "Una dompna soiseubuda" a borrowed lady or as the Italians translated it "Una donna ideale."

Tho thou well dost wish me ill
                        Audiart, Audiart,
Where thy bodice laces start
As ivy fingers clutching thru
Its crevices,
                Audiart, Audiart,
Stately, tall and lovely tender
Who shall render
                Audiart, Audiart
Praises meet unto thy fashion?
Here a word kiss!
            Pass I on
Unto Lady "Miels-de-Ben,"
Having praised thy girdle's scope,
How the stays ply back from it;
I breathe no hope
That thou shouldst . . . .
               Nay no whit
Bespeak thyself for anything.
Just a word in thy praise, girl,
Just for the swirl
Thy satins make upon the stair,
'Cause never a flaw was there

Where thy torse and limbs are met:
Tho thou hate me, read it set
In rose and gold,*
Or when the minstrel, tale half told
Shall burst to lilting at the phrase
        "Audiart, Audiart" . . . .

Bertrans, master of his lays,
Bertrans of Aultaforte thy praise
Sets forth, and tho thou hate me well,
Yea tho thou wish me ill
        Audiart, Audiart
Thy loveliness is here writ till,
        Audiart,
Oh, till thou come again.**
And being bent and wrinkled, in a form
That hath no perfect limning, when the warm
Youth dew is cold
Upon thy hands, and thy old soul
Scorning a new, wry'd casement
Churlish at seemed misplacement
Finds the earth as bitter
As now seems it sweet,
Being so young and fair
As then only in dreams,
Being then young and wry'd,
Broken of ancient pride
Thou shalt then soften
Knowing I know not how
Thou wert once she
        Audiart, Audiart
For whose fairness one forgave
        Audiart, Audiart
Que be-m vols mal.

* i. e. in illumed manuscript.
** reincarnate.

14

VILLONAUD FOR THIS YULE

Towards the Noel that morte saison
(Christ make the shepherds' homage dear!)
Then when the grey wolves everychone
Drink of the winds their chill small-beer
And lap o' the snows food's gueredon
Then makyth my heart his yule-tide cheer
(Skoal! with the dregs if the clear be gone!)
Wineing the ghosts of yester-year.

Ask ye what ghosts I dream upon?
(What of the magians' scented gear?)
The ghosts of dead loves everyone
That make the stark winds reek with fear
Lest love return with the foison sun
And slay the memories that me cheer
(Such as I drink to mine fashion)
Wineing the ghosts of yester-year.

Where are the joys my heart had won?
(Saturn and Mars to Zeus drawn near!) *
Where are the lips mine lay upon,
Aye! where are the glances feat and clear
That bade my heart his valor don?
I skoal to the eyes as grey-blown mere
(Who knows whose was that paragon?)
Wineing the ghosts of yester-year.

Prince: ask me not what I have done
Nor what God hath that can me cheer
But ye ask first where the winds are gone
Wineing the ghosts of yester-year.

    * *signum Nativitatis.*

A VILLONAUD. BALLAD OF THE GIBBET

Or the Song of the Sixth Companion

(Scene: *"En cest bourdel où tenons nostre estat"*)
It being remembered that there were six of us with Master
Villon, when that expecting presently to be hanged he writ a
ballad whereof ye know:
"Frères humains qui après nous vivez."

Drink ye a skoal for the gallows tree!
François and Margot and thee and me,
Drink we the comrades merrily
That said us, "Till then" for the gallows tree!

Fat Pierre with the hook gauche-main,
Thomas Larron "Ear-the-less,"
Tybalde and that armouress
Who gave this poignard its premier stain
Pinning the Guise that had been fain
To make him a mate of the "Hault Noblesse"
And bade her be out with ill address
As a fool that mocketh his drue's disdeign.

Drink we a skoal for the gallows tree!
François and Margot and thee and me,
Drink we to Marienne Ydole,
That hell brenn not her o'er cruelly.

Drink we the lusty robbers twain,
Black is the pitch o' their wedding dress,*
Lips shrunk back for the wind's caress
As lips shrink back when we feel the strain
Of love that loveth in hell's disdeign
And sense the teeth thru the lips that press
'Gainst our lips for the soul's distress
That striveth to ours across the pain.

* Certain gibbeted corpses used to be coated with tar as a preservative; thus
one scare crow served as warning for considerable time. See Hugo "L'Homme
qui Rit."

Drink we skoal to the gallows tree!
François and Margot and thee and me,
For Jehan and Raoul de Vallerie
Whose frames have the night and its winds in fee.

Maturin, Guillaume, Jacques d'Allmain,
Culdou lacking a coat to bless
One lean moiety of his nakedness
That plundered St. Hubert back o' the fane:
Aie! the lean bare tree is widowed again
For Michault le Borgne that would confess
In "faith and troth" to a traitoress
"Which of his brothers had he slain?"

But drink we skoal to the gallows tree!
François and Margot and thee and me:

These that we loved shall God love less
And smite alway at their faibleness?

Skoal!! to the Gallows! and then pray we:
God damn his hell out speedily
And bring their souls to his "Haulte Citee."

MESMERISM

"And a cat's in the water-butt"
Robt. Browning, *Mesmerism*

Aye you're a man that! ye old mesmerizer
Tyin' your meanin' in seventy swadelin's,
One must of needs be a hang'd early riser
To catch you at worm turning. Holy Odd's bodykins!

"Cat's i' the water butt!" Thought's in your verse-barrel,
Tell us this thing rather, then we'll believe you,
You, Master Bob-Browning, spite your apparel
Jump to your sense and give praise as we'd lief do.

You wheeze as a head-cold long-tonsilled Calliope,
But God! what a sight you ha' got o' our innards,
Mad as a hatter but surely no Myope,
Broad as all ocean and leanin' man-kin'ards.

Heart that was big as the bowels of Vesuvius,
Words that were wing'd as her sparks in eruption,
Eagled and thundered as Jupiter Pluvius,
Sound in your wind past all signs o' corruption.

Here's to you, Old Hippety-hop o'the accents,
True to the Truth's sake and crafty dissector,
You grabbed at the gold sure; had no need to pack cents
Into your versicles.
                    Clear sight's elector!

FIFINE ANSWERS

> "Why is it that, disgraced, they seem to relish life the more?"
> *Fifine at the Fair*, VII, 5.

"Sharing his exile that hath borne the flame,
Joining his freedom that hath drunk the shame
And known the torture of the Skull-place hours
Free and so bound, that mingled with the powers
Of air and sea and light his soul's far reach
Yet strictured did the body-lips beseech
"To drink": "I thirst." And then the sponge of gall.

Wherefor we wastrels that the grey road's call
Doth master and make slaves and yet make free,
Drink all of life and quaffing lustily
Take bitter with the sweet without complain
And sharers in his drink defy the pain
That makes you fearful to unfurl your souls.

We claim no glory. If the tempest rolls
About us we have fear, and then
Having so small a stake grow bold again.
We know not definitely even this
But 'cause some vague half knowing half doth miss
Our consciousness and leaves us feeling
That somehow all is well, that sober, reeling
From the last carouse, or in what measure
Of so called right or so damned wrong our leisure
Runs out uncounted sand beneath the sun,
That, spite your carping, still the thing is done
With some deep sanction, that, we know not how,
Without our thought gives feeling; You allow
That 'tis not need we *know* our every thought
Or see the work shop where each mask is wrought
Wherefrom we view the world of box and pit,
Careless of wear, just so the mask shall fit
And serve our jape's turn for a night or two.

Call! eh bye! the little door at twelve!

I meet you there myself.

ANIMA SOLA

> "Then neither is the bright orb of the sun greeted nor yet
> either the shaggy might of earth or sea, thus then, in the firm
> vessel of harmony is fixed God, a sphere, round, rejoicing in
> complete solitude."
>
> Empedokles

Exquisite loneliness
Bound of mine own caprice
I fly on the wings of an unknown chord
  That ye hear not,
  Can not discern

My music is weird and untamed
Barbarous, wild, extreme,
I fly on the note that ye hear not
On the chord that ye can not dream.
And lo, your out-worn harmonies are behind me
     As ashes and mouldy bread,
I die in the tears of the morning
     I kiss the wail of the dead.
My joy is the wind of heaven,
     My drink is the gall of night,
My love is the light of meteors;
     The autumn leaves in flight.

I pendant sit in the vale of fate
    I twine the Maenad strands
And lo, the three Eumenides
     Take justice at my hands.
For I fly in the gale of an unknown chord.
The blood of light is God's delight
And I am the life blood's ward.

O Loneliness, O Loneliness,
Thou boon of the fires blown
From heaven to hell and back again
Thou cup of the God-man's own!

For I am a weird untamed
That eat of no man's meat
My house is the rain ye wail against
     My drink is the wine of sleet.

My music is your disharmony
     Intangible, most mad,
For the clang of a thousand cymbals
Where the sphinx smiles o'er the sand,
     And viol strings that out-sing kings
Are the least of my command.
Exquisite, alone, untrammeled
I kiss the nameless sign
And the laws of my inmost being
     Chant to the nameless shrine.

I flee on the wing of a note ye know not,
My music disowns your law,
Ye can not tread the road I wed

And lo! I refuse your bidding.
I will not bow to the expectation that ye have.
Lo! I am gone as a red flame into the mist,
My chord is unresolved by your counter-harmonies.

IN TEMPORE SENECTUTIS

        For we are old
And the earth passion dyeth;
We have watched him die a thousand times,
When he wanes an old wind cryeth,
        For we are old
And passion hath died for us a thousand times
        But we grew never weary.

Memory faileth, as the lotus-loved chimes
        Sink into fluttering of wind,
        But we grow never weary
        For we are old.

The strange night-wonder of your eyes
Dies not, tho passion flyeth
        Along the star fields of Arcturus
And is no more unto our hands;
        My lips are cold
And yet we twain are never weary,
And the strange night-wonder is upon us,
The leaves hold our wonder in their flutterings,
The wind fills our mouths with strange words
        For our wonder that grows not old.

The moth hour of our day is upon us
        Holding the dawn;
There is strange Night-wonder in our eyes
Because the Moth-Hour leadeth the dawn
As a maiden, holding her fingers,
The rosy, slender fingers of the dawn.

He: "Red spears bore the warrior dawn
                    "Of old.
    "Strange! Love, hast thou forgotten
            "The red spears of the dawn,
            "The pennants of the morning?"

She: "Nay, I remember, but now
        "Cometh the Dawn, and the Moth-Hour
        "Together with him; softly
          "For we are old."

FAMAM LIBROSQUE CANO

Your songs?
            Oh! The little mothers
Will sing them in the twilight,
And when the night
Shrinketh the kiss of the dawn
That loves and kills,
What time the swallow fills
Her note, then the little rabbit folk
That some call children,
Such as are up and wide
Will laugh your verses to each other,
Pulling on their shoes for the day's business,
Serious child business that the world
Laughs at, and grows stale;
Such is the tale
—Part of it—of thy song-life.

Mine?

A book is known by them that read
That same. Thy public in my screed
Is listed. Well! Some score years hence
Behold mine audience,
As we had seen him yesterday.

Scrawny, be-spectacled, out at heels,
Such an one as the world feels
A sort of curse against its guzzling
And its age-lasting wallow for red greed
And yet; full speed
Tho it should run for its own getting,
Will turn aside to sneer at
'Cause he hath
No coin, no will to snatch the aftermath
Of Mammon.
Such an one as women draw away from
For the tobacco ashes scattered on his coat
And sith his throat
Shows razor's unfamiliarity
And three days' beard;

Such an one picking a ragged
Backless copy from the stall,
Too cheap for cataloguing,
Loquitur,

"Ah-eh! the strange rare name . . . .
"Ah-eh! He must be rare if even *I* have not . . . ."
And lost mid-page
Such age
As his pardons the habit,
He analyzes form and thought to see
How I 'scaped immortality.

THE CRY OF THE EYES

Rest Master, for we be aweary, weary
And would feel the fingers of the wind
Upon these lids that lie over us
Sodden and lead-heavy.

Rest brother, for lo! the dawn is without!
The yellow flame paleth
And the wax runs low.

Free us, for without be goodly colors,
Green of the wood-moss and flower colors,
And coolness beneath the trees.

Free us, for we perish
In this ever-flowing monotony
Of ugly print marks, black
Upon white parchment.

Free us, for there is one
Whose smile more availeth
Than all the age-old knowledge of thy books:
And we would look thereon.

SCRIPTOR IGNOTUS

To K. R. H.
Ferrara 1715

"When I see thee as some poor song-bird
Battering its wings, against this cage we call Today,
Then would I speak comfort unto thee,
From out the heights I dwell in, when
That great sense of power is upon me
And I see my greater soul-self bending
Sibylwise with that great forty-year epic

That you know of, yet unwrit
But as some child's toy 'tween my fingers,
And see the sculptors of new ages carve me thus,
And model with the music of my couplets in their hearts:
Surely if in the end the epic
And the small kind deed are one;
If to God, the child's toy and the epic are the same.
E'en so, did one make a childs toy,
He might wright it well
And cunningly, that the child might
Keep it for his children's children
And all have joy thereof.

Dear, an this dream come true,
Then shall all men say of thee
"She 'twas that played him power at life's morn,
And at the twilight Evensong,
And God's peace dwelt in the mingled chords
She drew from out the shadows of the past,
And old world melodies that else
He had known only in his dreams
Of Iseult and of Beatrice.

Dear, an this dream come true,
I, who being poet only,
Can give thee poor words only,
Add this one poor other tribute,
This thing men call immortality.
A gift I give thee even as Ronsard gave it.
Seeing before time, one sweet face grown old,
And seeing the old eyes grow bright
From out the border of Her fire-lit wrinkles,
As she should make boast unto her maids
"Ronsard hath sung the beauty, *my* beauty,
                    Of the days that I was fair."

So hath the boon been given, by the poets of old time
(Dante to Beatrice,—an I profane not—)
Yet with my lesser power shall I not strive
                    To give it thee?

All ends of things are with Him
From whom are all things in their essence.
If my power be lesser
Shall my striving be less keen?
But rather more! if I would reach the goal,
    Take then the striving!
"And if," for so the Florentine hath writ
When having put all his heart
Into his "Youth's Dear Book"
He yet strove to do more honor
To that lady dwelling in his inmost soul,
He would wax yet greater
To make her earthly glory more.
Though sight of hell and heaven were
    price thereof,
If so it be His will, with whom
Are all things and through whom
Are all things good,
Will I make for thee and for the beauty of thy music
A new thing
As hath not heretofore been writ.
    Take then my promise!

Note. Bertold Lomax, English Dante scholar and mystic, died in Ferrara
1723, with his "great epic," still a mere shadow, a nebula crossed with some
few gleams of wonder light. The lady of the poem an organist of Ferrara, whose
memory has come down to us only in Lomax' notes.

DONZELLA BEATA

  Era mea
  In qua terra
  Dulce myrti floribus
   Rosa amoris
   Via erroris
  Ad te coram veniam?

Soul,
Caught in the rose-hued mesh
Of o'er fair earthly flesh,

Stooped you this thing to bear
Again for me? And be
Rare light to me, gold-white
In the shadowy path I tread?

Surely a bolder maid art thou
Than one in tearful, fearful longing
That should wait
Lily-cinctured at the gate
Of high heaven, Star-diadem'd,
Crying that I should come to thee.

VANA

In vain have I striven
        to teach my heart to bow;
In vain have I said to him
"There be many singers   greater than thou."

But his answer cometh,   as winds and as lutany,
As a vague crying upon the night
That leaveth me no rest,   saying ever,
                "Song,   a song."
Their echoes play upon each other in the twilight
Seeking ever a song.
Lo, I am worn with travail
And the wandering of many roads hath made my eyes
As dark red circles filled with dust.
Yet there is a trembling upon me in the twilight,
        And little red elf words   crying "A song,"
        Little grey elf words   crying for a song,
        Little brown leaf words   crying "A song,"
        Little green leaf words   crying for a song.
The words are as leaves, old brown leaves in the spring time
Blowing they know not whither, seeking a song.

LI BEL CHASTEUS

That castle stands the highest in the land
Far-seen and mighty.   Of the great hewn stones
What shall I say? And deep foss way
That far beneath us bore of old
A swelling turbid sea
Hill-born and torrent-wise
Unto the fields below, where
Staunch villein and wandered
Burgher held the land and tilled
Long labouring for gold of wheat grain
And to see the beards come forth
For barley's even tide.

But circle-arched, above the hum of life
We dwelt amid the ancient boulders,
Gods had hewn and druids runed
Unto that birth most wondrous, that had grown
A mighty fortress while the world had slept
And we awaited in the shadows there
While mighty hands had labored sightlessly
And shaped this wonder 'bove the ways of men
Me seems we could not see the great green waves
Nor rocky shore by Tintagoel
From this our hold,
But came faint murmuring as undersong
E'en as the burghers' hum arose
And died as faint wind melody
Beneath our gates.

THAT PASS BETWEEN THE FALSE DAWN
AND THE TRUE

Blown of the winds whose goal is "No-man-knows"
As feathered seeds upon the wind are borne,
To kiss as winds kiss and to melt as snows
And in our passing taste of all men's scorn,
Wraiths of a dream that fragrant ever blows
From out the night we know not to the morn,
Borne upon winds whose goal is "No-man-knows."
An hour to each! We greet. The hour flows
And joins its hue to mighty hues out-worn
Weaving the Perfect Picture, while we torn
Give cry in harmony, and weep the Rose
Blown of the winds whose goal is "No-man-knows."

IN MORTE DE

Oh wine-sweet ghost how are we borne apart
Of winds that restless blow we know not where
As little shadows smoke-wraith-sudden start
If music break the freighted dream of air;
So, fragile curledst thou in my dream-wracked heart,
So, sudden summoned dost thou leave it bare.
O wine-sweet ghost how are we borne apart!
As little flames amid the dead coal dart
And lost themselves upon some hidden stair,
So futile elfin be we well aware
Old cries I cry to thee as I depart,
"O wine-sweet ghost how are we borne apart."

THRENOS

No more for us the little sighing
No more the winds at twilight trouble us.

Lo the fair dead!

No more do I burn.
No more for us the fluttering of wings
That whirred the air above us.

Lo the fair dead!

No more desire flayeth me,
No more for us the trembling
At the meeting of hands.

Lo the fair dead!

No more for us the wine of the lips
No more for us the knowledge.

Lo the fair dead!

No more the torrent
No more for us the meeting-place
(Lo the fair dead!)
Tintagoel.

COMRADERIE

> "E tuttoque io fosse a la compagnia di molti, quanto alla
> vista."

Sometimes I feel thy cheek against my face
Close-pressing, soft as is the South's first breath
That all the subtle earth-things summoneth
To spring in wood-land and in meadow space.

Yea sometimes in a bustling man-filled place
Me seemeth some-wise thy hair wandereth
Across my eyes, as mist that halloweth
The air a while and giveth all things grace.

Or on still evenings when the rain falls close
There comes a tremor in the drops, and fast
My pulses run, knowing thy thought hath passed
That beareth thee as doth the wind a rose.

BALLAD ROSALIND

Our Lord is set in his great oak throne
For our old Lord liveth all alone
        These ten years and gone.

A book on his knees and bent his head
For our old Lord's love is long since dead.
        These ten years and gone.

For our young Lord Hugh went to the East,
And fought for the cross and is crows' feast
        These ten years and gone.

"But where is our Lady Rosalind,
Fair as day and fleet as wind
        These ten years and gone?"

For our old Lord broodeth all alone
Silent and grey in his black oak throne
        These ten years and gone.

Our old Lord broodeth silent there
For to question him none will dare
　　These ten years and more.

Where is our Lady Rosalind
Fair as dawn and fleet as wind.
　　These ten years and gone?

Our old Lord sits with never a word
And only the flame and the wind are heard
　　These ten years and more.

.　　.　　.　　.　　.　　.

"Father! I come," and she knelt at the throne,
"Father! know me, I am thine own.
　　"These ten years and more

"Have they kept me for ransom at Chastel d' Or
"And never a word have I heard from thee
　　"These ten years and more."

But our old Lord answered never a word
And only sobbing and wind were heard.
　　(These ten years and gone.)

We took our Lord and his great oak throne
And set them deep in a vault of stone
　　These ten years and gone,

A book on his knees and bow'd his head
For the Lord of our old Lord's love is dead
　　These ten years and gone,

And Lady Rosalind rules in his stead
(Thank we God for our daily bread)
　　These ten years and more.

MALRIN

Malrin, because of his jesting stood without, till all the guests were entered in unto the Lord's house. Then there came an angel unto him saying, "Malrin, why hast thou tarried?"

To whom, Malrin, "There is no feeding till the last sheep be gone into the fold. Wherefor I stayed chaffing the laggards and mayhap when it was easy helping the weak."

Saith the angel, "The Lord will be wroth with thee, Malrin, that thou art last."

"Nay sirrah!" quipped Malrin, "I knew my Lord when thou and thy wings were yet in the egg."

Saith the angel, "Peace! hasten lest there be no bread for thee, rattle-tongue."

"Ho," quoth Malrin, "is it thus that thou knowest my Lord? Aye! I am his fool and have felt his lash but meseems that thou hast set thy ignorance to my folly, saying 'Hasten lest there be an end to his bread.' "

Whereat the angel went in in wrath. And Malrin, turning slowly, beheld the last blue of twilight and the sinking of the silver of the stars. And the suns sank down like cooling gold in their crucibles, and there was a murmuring amid the azure curtains and far clarions from the keep of heaven, as a Muezzin crying, "Allah akbar, Allah il Allah! *it is finished.*"

And Malrin beheld the broidery of the stars become as wind-worn tapestries of ancient wars. And the memory of all old songs swept by him as an host blue-robèd trailing in dream, Odysseus, and Tristram, and the pale great gods of storm, the mailed Campeador and Roland and Villon's women and they of Valhalla; as a cascade of dull sapphires so poured they out of the mist and were gone. And above him the stronger clarion as a Muezzin crying "Allah akbar, Allah il Allah, *it is finished.*"

And again Malrin, drunk as with the dew of old world druidings, was bowed in dream. And the third dream of Malrin was the dream of the seven and no man knoweth it.

And a third time came the clarion and after it the Lord called softly unto Malrin, "Son, why hast thou tarried? Is it not fulfilled, thy dream and mine?"

And Malrin, "O Lord, I am thy fool and thy love hath been my scourge and my wonder, my wine and mine extasy. But one left me awroth and went in unto thy table. I tarried till his anger was blown out."

"Oh Lord for the ending of our dream I kiss thee. For his anger is with the names of Deirdre and Ysolt. And our dream is ended, PADRE."

MASKS

These tales of old disguisings, are they not
Strange myths of souls that found themselves among
Unwonted folk that spake an hostile tongue,
Some soul from all the rest who'd not forgot
The star-span acres of a former lot
Where boundless mid the clouds his course he swung,
Or carnate with his elder brothers sung
Ere ballad-makers lisped of Camelot?

Old singers half-forgetful of their tunes,
Old painters color-blind come back once more,
Old poets skill-less in the wind-heart runes,
Old wizards lacking in their wonder-lore:

All they that with strange sadness in their eyes
Ponder in silence o'er earth's queynt devyse?

ON HIS OWN FACE IN A GLASS

O strange face there in the glass!

O ribald company, O saintly host!
O sorrow-swept my fool,

What answer?
                    O ye myriad
That strive and play and pass,
Jest, challenge, counterlie,

I   ?   I   ?   I   ?
                                    And ye?

THE TREE

        I stood still and was a tree amid the wood
Knowing the truth of things unseen before,
Of Daphne and the laurel bow
And that god-feasting couple olde
That grew elm-oak amid the wold.
'Twas not until the gods had been
Kindly entreated and been brought within
Unto the hearth of their heart's home
That they might do this wonder-thing.
Nathless I have been a tree amid the wood
And many new things understood
That were rank folly to my head before.

INVERN

Earth's winter cometh
And I being part of all
And sith the spirit of all moveth in me
I must needs bear earth's winter
Drawn cold and grey with hours

And joying in a momentary sun,
Lo I am withered with waiting till my spring cometh!
Or crouch covetous of warmth
O'er scant-logged ingle blaze,
Must take cramped joy in tomed Longinus
That, read I him first time
The woods agleam with summer
Or mid desirous winds of spring,
Had set me singing spheres
Or made heart to wander forth among warm roses
Or curl in grass nest neath a kindly moon.

PLOTINUS

As one that would draw thru the node of things,
    Back sweeping to the vortex of the cone,
    Cloistered about with memories, alone
In chaos, while the waiting silence sings:

Obliviate of cycles' wanderings
  I was an atom on creation's throne
  And knew all nothing my unconquered own.
God! Should I be the hand upon the strings?!

But I was lonely as a lonely child.
I cried amid the void and heard no cry,
And then for utter loneliness, made I
New thoughts as crescent images of *me*.
And with them was my essence reconciled
While fear went forth from mine eternity.

PROMETHEUS

For we be the beaten wands
And the bearers of the flame.
    Our selves have died lang syne, and we
Go ever upward as the sparks of light
Enkindling all
'Gainst whom our shadows fall.

Weary to sink, yet ever upward borne,
Flame, flame that riseth ever
To the flame within the sun,
Tearing our casement ever
For the way is one
That beareth upward
To the flame within the sun.

AEGUPTON

I—even I—am he who knoweth the roads
Thru the sky and the wind thereof is my body.

I have beheld the Lady of Life.
I, even I, that fly with the swallows.

Green and grey is her raiment
Trailing along the wind.

I—even I—am he who knoweth the roads
Thru the sky and the wind thereof is my body.

Manus animam pinxit—
My pen is in my hand

To write the acceptable word,
My mouth to chaunt the pure singing:

Who hath the mouth to receive it?
The Song of the Lotus of Kumi?

I—even I—am he who knoweth the roads
Thru the sky and the wind thereof is my body.

I am flame that riseth in the sun,
I, even I, that fly with the swallows

For the moon is upon my forehead,
The winds are under my kiss.

The moon is a great pearl in the waters of sapphire;
Cool to my fingers the flowing waters.

I—even I—am he who knoweth the roads
Of the sky and the wind thereof is my body.

I will return unto the halls of the flowing
Of the truth of the children of Ashu.

I—even I—am he who knoweth the roads
Of the sky and the wind thereof is my body.

BALLAD FOR GLOOM

For God, our God, is a gallant foe
That playeth behind the veil.

I have loved my God as a child at heart
That seeketh deep bosoms for rest,
I have loved my God as maid to man
But lo this thing is best:

To love your God as a gallant foe
                    that plays behind the veil,
To meet your God as the night winds meet
                    beyond Arcturus' pale.

I have played with God for a woman,
I have staked with my God for truth,
I have lost to my God as a man, clear eyed,
        His dice be not of ruth,

For I am made as a naked blade
        But hear ye this thing in sooth:

Who loseth to God as man to man
        Shall win at the turn of the game.
I have drawn my blade where the lightnings meet
        But the ending is the same:
Who loseth to God as the sword blades lose
        Shall win at the end of the game.

For God, our God, is a gallant foe
                    that playeth behind the veil
Whom God deigns not to overthrow
                    Hath need of triple mail.

FOR E. McC.

> That was my counter-blade under Leonardo Terrone, Master
> of Fence.

Gone while your tastes were keen to you,
Gone where the grey winds call to you,
By that high fencer, even Death,
Struck of the blade that no man parrieth,
Such is your fence, one saith,
        one that hath known you.

Drew you your sword most gallantly
Made you your pass most valiantly
      'Gainst that grey fencer, even Death.

Gone as a gust of breath.
Faith! no man tarrieth,
"Se il cor ti manca," but it failed thee not!
"Non ti fidar," it is the sword that speaks
"In me." *
Thou trusted'st in thyself and met the blade
'Thout mask or gauntlet, and art laid
As memorable broken blades that be
Kept as bold trophies of old pageantry,
As old Toledos past their days of war
Are kept mnemonic of the strokes they bore,
So art thou with us, being good to keep
In our heart's sword-rack, tho thy sword-arm sleep.

ENVOI

Struck of the blade that no man parrieth
Pierced of the point that toucheth lastly all,
'Gainst that grey fencer, even Death,
Behold the shield! He shall not take thee all.

SALVE O PONTIFEX!

To Swinburne; an hemichaunt

One after one do they leave thee,
      High Priest of Iacchus,
Toning thy melodies even as winds tone
The whisper of tree leaves, on sun-lit days.
Even as the sands are many

* Sword-rune "If thy heart fail thee trust not in me."

40

And the seas beyond the sands are one
In ultimate; So we here being many
Are unity. Nathless thy compeers
          Knowing thy melody,
Lulled with the wine of thy music
Go seaward silently, leaving thee sentinel
O'er all the mysteries,
          High Priest of Iacchus,
For the lines of life lie under thy fingers,
And above the vari-colored strands
Thine eyes look out unto the infinitude
Of the blue waves of heaven,
And even as Triplex Sisterhood
Thou fingerest the threads knowing neither
Cause nor the ending.
          High Priest of Iacchus
Draw'st forth a multiplicity
Of strands, and beholding
The color thereof, raisest thy voice
Toward the sunset,
          O High Priest of Iacchus!
And out of the secrets of the inmost mysteries
Thou chantest strange far-sourced canticles;
          O High Priest of Iacchus!
Life and the ways of Death her
Twin born sister, being Life's counterpart
(And evil being inversion of blessing
That blessing herself might have being)
And night and the winds of night;
Silent voices ministering to the souls
Of hamadryads that hold council concealed
In streams and tree-shadowing
Forests on hill slopes,
          O High Priest of Iacchus
All the manifold mystery
Thou makest wine of song of,
And maddest thy following
Even with visions of great deeds
And their futility, and the worship of love,
          O High Priest of Iacchus.

Wherefor tho thy co-novices bent to the scythe
Of the magian wind that is voice of Prosephone,
Leaving thee solitary, master of initiating
Maenads that come thru the
Vine-entangled ways of the forest
Seeking, out of all the world
       Madness of Iacchus,
That being skilled in the secrets of the double cup
They might turn the dead of the world
Into beauteous paeans,
       O High Priest of Iacchus
Wreathed with the glory of years of creating
Entangled music that men may not
Over readily understand:
             Breathe!
Now that evening cometh upon thee,
Breathe upon us that low-bowed and exultant
Drink wine of Iacchus
       That since the conquering *
Hath been chiefly contained in the numbers
Of them that even as thou, have woven
Wicker baskets for grape clusters
Wherein is concealèd the source of the vintage,
       O High Priest of Iacchus
Breathe thou upon us
       Thy magic in parting!
Even as they thy co-novices
Being mingled with the sea
While yet thou mad'st canticles
Serving upright before the altar
That is bound about with shadows
Of dead years wherein thy Iacchus
Looked not upon the hills, that being
Uncared for, praised not him in entirety,
       O High Priest of Iacchus
Being now near to the border of the sands
Where the sapphire girdle of the sea
       Encinctureth the maiden

* Vicisti, Nazarenus!

42

Prosephone, released for the spring.
Look! Breathe upon us
The wonder of the thrice encinctured mystery
Whereby thou being full of years art young,
Loving even this lithe Prosephone
That is free for the seasons of plenty;

Whereby thou being young art old
And shalt stand before this Prosephone
        Whom thou lovest,
In darkness, even at that time
That she being returned to her husband
Shall be queen and a maiden no longer,

Wherein thou being neither old nor young,
Standing on the verge of the sea
Shalt pass from being sand,
        O High Priest of Iacchus,
And becoming wave
        Shalt encircle all sands,
Being transmuted thru all
The girdling of the sea.
        O High Priest of Iacchus,
Breathe thou upon us!

TO THE DAWN: DEFIANCE

Ye blood-red spears-men of the dawn's array
That drive my dusk-clad knights of dream away,
Hold! For I will not yield.

My moated soul shall dream in your despite
A refuge for the vanquished hosts of night
That *can* not yield.

THE DECADENCE

Tarnished we! Tarnished! Wastrels all!
And yet the art goes on, goes on.
Broken our strength, yea as crushed reeds we fall,
And yet the art, the *art* goes on.

Bearers of beauty flame and wane,
The sunset shadow and the rose's bloom.
The sapphire seas grow dull to shine again
As new day glistens in the old day's room.

Broken our manhood for the wrack and strain;
Drink of our hearts the sunset and the cry
"Io Triumphe!" Tho our lips be slain
We see Art vivant, and exult to die.

REDIVIVUS

Hail Michael Agnolo! my soul lay slain
Or else in torpor such, death seems more fair,
I looked upon the light, if light were there
I knew it not. There seemed not any pain,
Nor joy, nor thought nor glorious deed nor strain
Of any song that half remembered were
For sign of quickness in that soul; but bare
Gaunt walls alone me seemed it to remain.

Thou praisest Dante well, My Lord: "No tongue
"Can tell of him what told of him should be
"For on blind eyes his splendor shines too strong."
If so his soul goes on unceasingly
Shall mine own flame count flesh one life too long
To hold its light and bear ye company?

44

FISTULAE

"To make her madrigal
"Who shall the rose sprays bring;
"To make her madrigal
"And bid my heart to sing?"

SONG

Love thou thy dream
All base love scorning,
Love thou the wind
And here take warning
That dreams alone can truly be,
For 'tis in dream I come to thee.

MOTIF

I have heard a wee wind searching
Thru still forests for me,
I have seen a wee wind searching
                    O'er still sea.

Thru woodlands dim
                    Have I taken my way,
And o'er silent waters, night and day
Have I sought the wee wind.

LA REGINA AVRILLOUSE

Lady of rich allure,
Queen of the spring's embrace,
Your arms are long like boughs of ash,
Mid laugh broken streams, spirit of rain unsure,
Breath of the poppy flower,
All the wood thy bower
        And the hills thy dwelling place.

This will I no more dream,
Warm is thine arm's allure
Warm is the gust of breath
That ere thy lips meet mine
Kisseth my cheek and saith:
"This is the joy of earth,
Here is the wine of mirth
        Drain ye one goblet sure,

Take ye the honey cup
The honied song raise up,
Drink of the spring's allure
April and dew and rain,
Brown of the earth sing sure,
Cheeks and lips and hair
And soft breath that kisseth where
        Thy lips have come not yet to drink."

Moss and the mold of earth
These be thy couch of mirth,
Long arms thy boughs of shade
April-alluring, as the blade
Of grass doth catch the dew
And make it crown to hold the sun,
Banner be you
        Above my head
Glory to all wold display'd
        April-alluring, glory-bold.

A ROUSE

Save ye, Merry gentlemen! Vagabonds and Rovers,
        Hell take the hin'most,
        We're for the clovers!
"Soul" sings the preacher.

Our joy's the light.
"Goal" bawls ambition.
Grass our delight!

Save ye, merry gentlemen!
Whirr and dew of earth,
Beauty 'thout raiment,
Reed pipes and mellow mirth
Scot free, no payment!

Gods be for heaven,
Clay the poet's birth!
Save ye merry gentlemen!
Wind and dew and spray o' sea
Hell take the hin'most,
Foot or sail for Arcady
Voice o' lark and breath of bee
Hell take the hin'most!
Our drink shall be the orange wine,
House o' boughs and roof o' vine
Hell take the hin'most!
Laugh and lips and gleam o' hair
Fore-kiss breath, and shoulders bare,
Save you queen o April!

(La Regina Avrillouse loquitur).

Follow! follow!

Breath of mirth,
My bed, my bower green of earth,
Naught else hath any worth.
Save ye "jolif bachillier"!
Hell take the hin'most!

NICOTINE

A Hymn to the Dope

Goddess of the murmuring courts,
      Nicotine, my Nicotine,
Houri of the mystic sports,
      trailing-robed in gabardine,
Gliding where the breath hath glided,
Hidden sylph of filmy veils,
Truth behind the dream is veiléd
E'en as thou art, smiling ever, ever gliding,
Wraith of wraiths, dim lights dividing
Purple, grey, and shadow green
      Goddess, Dream-grace, Nicotine.

Goddess of the shadow's lights,
      Nicotine, my Nicotine,
Some would set old Earth to rights,
      Thou and I none such I ween.
Veils of shade our dream dividing,
Houris dancing, intergliding,
Wraith of wraiths and dream of faces,
Silent guardian of the old unhallowed places,
Utter symbol of all old sweet druidings,
Mem'ry of witched wold and green,
      Nicotine, my Nicotine:

Neath the shadows of thy weaving
Dreams that need no undeceiving,
Loves that longer hold me not,
Dreams I dream not any more,
Fragrance of old sweet forgotten places,
Smiles of dream-lit, flit-by faces
All as perfume Arab-sweet
Deck the high road to thy feet

As were Godiva's coming fated
And all the April's blush belated

Were lain before her, carpeting
The stones of Coventry with spring,
So thou my mist-enwreathéd queen,
Nicotine, white Nicotine,
          Riding engloried in thy hair
Mak'st by-road of our dreams
          Thy thorough-fare.

IN TEMPORE SENECTUTIS

(An Anti-stave for Dowson)

When I am old
I will not have you look apart
From me, into the cold,
Friend of my heart,
Nor be sad in your remembrance
Of the careless, mad-heart semblance
That the wind hath blown away
When I am old.

When I am old
And the white hot wonder-fire
Unto the world seem cold,
My soul's desire
Know you then that all life's shower,
The rain of the years, that hour
Shall make blow for us one flower,
Including all, when we are old.

When I am old
If you remember
Any love save what is then
Hearth light unto life's December
Be your joy of past sweet chalices

To know then naught but this
"How many wonders are less sweet
Than love I bear to thee
When I am old."

OLTRE LA TORRE: ROLANDO

There dwelt a lady in a tower high,
Foul beasts surrounded it,
I scattered them and left her free.

O-la! Oll-aa! The green-wood tree
Hath many a smooth sward under it!

My lady hath a long red cloak,
Her robe was of the sun,
This blade hath broke a baron's yoke,
That hath such guerdon won.

Yea I have broke my Lord Gloom's yoke
New yoke will I have none,
Save the yoke that shines in the golden bow
Betwixt the rain and the sun.

Ol-la! Ol-la! the good green-wood!
The good green wood is free!
Say who will lie in the bracken high
And laugh, and laugh for the winds with me?

Make-strong old dreams lest this our world lose heart.

> For man is a skinfull of wine
> But his soul is a hole full of God
> And the song of all time blows thru him
> As winds thru a knot-holed board.
>
> Tho man be a skin full of wine
> Yet his heart is a little child
> That croucheth low beneath the wind
> When the God-storm battereth wild.

A QUINZAINE FOR THIS YULE
1908

A QUINZAINE FOR THIS YULE

Being selected from a
Venetian sketch-book
—"San Trovaso"—

— BY —
EZRA POUND

Front cover of A Quinzaine for This Yule, *London, 1908*

Beauty should never be presented explained. It is Marvel and Wonder, and in art we should find first these doors—Marvel and Wonder—and, coming through them, a slow understanding (slow even though it be a succession of lightning understandings and perceptions) as of a figure in mist, that still and ever gives to each one his own right of believing, each after his own creed and fashion.

Always the desire to know and to understand more deeply must precede any reception of beauty. Without holy curiosity and awe none find her, and woe to that artist whose work wears its "heart on its sleeve."

WESTON ST. LLEWMYS

PRELUDE: OVER THE OGNISANTI

High-dwelling 'bove the people here,
Being alone with beauty most the while,
Lonely?
                How can I be,
Having mine own great thoughts for paladins
Against all gloom and woe and every bitterness?

Also have I the swallows and the sunset
And I see much life below me,
                In the garden, on the waters,
And hither float the shades of songs they sing
To sound of wrinkled mandolin, and plash of waters,
Which shades of song re-echoed
Within that somewhile barren hall, my heart,
Are found as I transcribe them following.

NIGHT LITANY

O Dieu, purifiez nos coeurs!
        purifiez nos coeurs!

Yea the lines hast thou laid unto me
        in pleasant places,
And the beauty of this thy Venice
        hast thou shewn unto me
Until is its loveliness become unto me
        a thing of tears.

O God, what great kindness
        have we done in times past
        and forgotten it,
That thou givest this wonder unto us,
        O God of waters?

O God of the night
        What great sorrow
Cometh unto us,
        That thou thus repayest us
Before the time of its coming?

O God of silence,
        Purifiez nos coeurs
        Purifiez nos coeurs
For we have seen
The glory of the shadow of the
    likeness of thine handmaid,
Yea, the glory of the shadow
    of thy Beauty hath walked
Upon the shadow of the waters
    In this thy Venice.
        And before the holiness
Of the shadow of thy handmaid
    Have I hidden mine eyes,
        O God of waters.

O God of silence,
             Purifiez nos coeurs,
             Purifiez nos coeurs,
O God of waters,
             make clean our hearts within us
And our lips to show forth thy praise,
             For I have seen the
shadow of this thy Venice
floating upon the waters,
             And thy stars
have seen this thing out of their far courses
have they seen this thing,
             O God of waters.
Even as are thy stars
Silent unto us in their far-coursing,
Even so is mine heart
             become silent within me.

(Fainter)
             Purifiez nos coeurs
O God of the silence,
             Purifiez nos coeurs
O God of waters.

PURVEYORS GENERAL

Praise to the lonely ones!
Give praise out of your ease
To them whom the farther seas
Bore out from amongst you.

We, that through all the world
Have wandered seeking new things
And quaint tales, that your ease

May gather such dreams as please
        you, the Home-stayers.

We, that through chaos have hurled
Our souls riven and burning,
Torn, mad, even as windy seas
Have we been, that your ease
Should keep bright amongst you:

That new tales and strange peoples
Such as the further seas
Wash on the shores of,
That new mysteries and increase
Of sunlight should be amongst you,
        you, the home-stayers.

Even for these things, driven from you,
Have we, drinking the utmost lees
Of all the world's wine and sorrowing
Gone forth from out your ease,
        And borrowing
Out of all lands and realms
        of the infinite,
New tales, new mysteries,
New songs from out the breeze
That maketh soft the far evenings,
Have brought back these things
        Unto your ease,
Yours unto whom peace is given.

AUBE OF THE WEST DAWN.
VENETIAN JUNE

From the Tale "How Malrin chose for his Lady the reflection of the Dawn and was thereafter true to her."

When svelte the dawn reflected in the west,
As did the sky slip off her robes of night,
I see to stand mine armouress confessed,
Then doth my spirit know himself aright,
And tremulous against her faint-flushed breast
Doth cast him quivering, her bondsman quite.

When I the dawn reflected in the west,
Fragile and maiden to my soul have pressed,
Pray I, her mating hallowed in God's sight,
That none asunder me with bale of might
From her whose lips have bade mine own be blest,
My bride, "The dawn reflected in the west."

I think from such perceptions as this arose the ancient myths of the demi-gods; as from such as that in "The Tree" (*A Lume Spento*), the myths of metamorphosis.

TO LA CONTESSA BIANZAFIOR (CENT. XIV)

(Defense at Parting)

I

And all who read these lines shall love her then
Whose laud is all their burthen, and whose praise
Is in my heart forever, tho' my lays
But stumble and grow startled dim again
When I would bid them, mid the courts of men,
Stand and take judgment. Whoso in new days
Shall read this script, or wander in the ways
My heart hath gone, shall praise her then.

Knowing this thing, "White Flower," I bid thy thought
Turn toward what thing a singer's love should be;
Stood I within thy gates and went not on,
One poor fool's love were all thy gueredon.
I go—my song upon the winds set free—
And lo!
      A thousand souls to thine are brought.

II
"This fellow mak'th his might seem over strong!"

Hath there a singer trod our dusty ways
And left not twice this hoard to weep her praise,
Whose name was made the glory of his song?

Hear ye, my peers! Judge ye, if I be wrong.
Hath Lesbia more love than all Catullus' days
Should've counted her of love? Tell me where strays
Her poet now, what ivory gates among?

Think ye? Ye think it not; my vaunt o'er bold?
Hath Deirdre, or Helen, or Beatrys,
More love than to maid unsung there is?

Be not these other hearts, when his is cold,
That seek thy soul with ardor manifold,
A better thing than were the husk of his?

III *
Whose is the gift of love? Tell me, whose is
The right to give or take? The thing is mine?
Think ye, O fools! It is not mine nor thine
Though I should strive, and I might strive y-wis,
Though I should strive what would we make o' this
Love for her soul, a love toward the divine,
A might within what heart that seeks such wine
As is the love betwixt her lips and his?

* [This, and part IV following, were omitted from *A Quinzaine for This Yule*, perhaps because of space limitations. They are printed here from the San Trovaso Notebook, thus explaining—and eliminating—the cryptic "III" and "IV" that appeared below part II on page 14 of the original printing.]

Were I to stand alone and guard this drink
To shut it off from such as come to pray,
What were the gueredon I bid ye think
To one that strove to hold the sun in goal?
Know ye first love, then come to me and say,
"Thou art inconstant and hast shamed thy soul."

IV

Night and the wax wanes. Night, and the text grows dim.
Who hath more love? Who brings more love?
    Speak strait.
Sung? Or unsung? Wedded? Or maid to wait
A thousand hearts who at the rune of him
That saw thy soul amid the Seraphim
Shall bear their incense to the horny gate
Whereby true dreams arise and hold their state?

Ye mock the lines. Pardon a poor fool's whim.

I, that have seen amid the dreams so much,
Speak dimly, stumble and draw forth your scorn.
Whether availeth more one prisoned man
Giving such labor as a bonds-man can,
Or a host of vagrants crying the morn
With "Hail" and "Day's grace" from the hearts o' such.

                        "queren lo jorn"

PARTENZA DI VENEZIA

Ne'er felt I parting from a woman loved
As feel I now my going forth from thee,
Yea, all thy waters cry out "Stay with me!"
And laugh reflected flames up luringly.

O elf-tale land that I three months have known,
Venice of dreams, if where the storm-wrack drave
As some uncertain ghost upon the wave,
For cloud thou hidest and then fitfully
For light and half-light feign'st reality,
If first we fear the dim dread of the unknown
Then reassured for the calm clear tone
"I am no spirit. Fear not me!"

As once the twelve storm-tossed on Galilee
Put off their fear yet came not nigh
Unto the holier mystery.
So we bewildered, yet have trust in thee,
And thus thou, Venice,

                      show'st thy mastery.

LUCIFER CADITURUS

By service clomb I heaven
And the law that smites the spheres,
Turning their courses even,
Served me as I serve God.

And shall all fears
Of chaos or this hell the Mover dreams—
Because *he knows* what is to me yet dim—
Bid me to plod
An huckster of the sapphire beams
From star to star
Giving to each his small embraced desire,
Shall I not bear this light
Unto what far
Unheavened bourne shall meet my fire
With some toward sympathy
That wills not rule?

By service clomb I heaven
And the Law served me, even
As I serve God; but shall this empery
Bid me restrict my course, or plod
A furrow worker in a space-set sod
Or turn the emeralds of the empyrean
Because I dread some pale remorse
Should gnaw the sinews of m' effulgent soul
Deigned I to break His bonds
        That hold the law?

SANDALPHON

And these about me die,
Because the pain of the infinite singing
Slayeth them.
Ye that have sung of the pain of the earth-horde's
        age-long crusading,
Ye know somewhat the strain,
        the sad-sweet wonder-pain of such singing.
And therefore ye know after what fashion
This singing hath power destroying.

Yea, these about me, bearing such song in homage
Unto the Mover of Circles,
Die for the might of their praising,
And the autumn of their marcescent wings
Maketh ever new loam for my forest;
And these grey ash trees hold within them
All the secrets of whatso things
They dreamed before their praises,
And in this grove my flowers,
Fruit of prayerful powers,
Have first their thought of life
        And then their being.

Ye marvel that I die not! *forsitan!*
Thinking me kin with such as may not weep,
Thinking me part of them that die for praising
—yea, tho' it be praising,
past the power of man's mortality to
dream or name its phases,
—yea, tho' it chaunt and paean
past the might of earth-dwelt
soul to think on,
—yea, tho' it be praising
as these the winged ones die of.

Ye think me one insensate
                else die I also
Sith these about me die,
and if I, watching
ever the multiplex jewel, of beryl and jasper
      and sapphire
Make of these prayers of earth ever new flowers;
Marvel and wonder!
Marvel and wonder even as I,
Giving to prayer new language
and causing the works to speak
of the earth-horde's age-lasting longing,
Even as I marvel and wonder, and know not,
Yet keep my watch in the ash wood.

Note on Sandalphon. The angel of prayer according to the Talmud stands unmoved among the angels of wind and fire, who die as their one song is finished; also as he gathers the prayers they turn to flowers in his hands.
Longfellow also treats of this, but as a legend rather than a reality.

FORTUNATUS

Resistless, unresisting, as some swift spear upon the flood
Follow'th the river's course and tarries not
But hath the stream's might for its on-sped own,
So towards my triumph, and so reads the will,
'Gainst which I will not, or mine eyes grow dim,
And dim they seem not, nor are willed to be.
For beauty greet'th them through your London rain,
That were of Adriatic beauty loved and won,
And though I seek all exile, yet my heart
Doth find new friends and all strange lands
Love me and grow my kin, and bid me speed.

Caught sometimes in the current of strange happiness, borne upon such winds as Dante beheld whirling the passion-pale shapes in the nether-gloom;* so here in the inner sunlight, or above cool, dew-green pasture lands, and again in caves of the azure magic.

WESTON ST. LLEWMYS

* *"E paion sì al vento esser leggieri."*
"Ombre portate dalla detta briga."

BEDDOESQUE

———— and going heavenward leaves
An opal spray to wake, a track that gleams
With new-old runes and magic of past time
Caught from the sea deep of the whole man-soul,
The "mantra" of our craft, that to the sun,
New brought and broken by the fearless keel,
That were but part of all the sun-smit sea,
Have for a space their individual being,
And do seem as things apart from all Time's hoard,
The great whole liquid jewel of God's truth.

GREEK EPIGRAM

Day and night are never weary,
Nor yet is God of creating
For day and night their torch-bearers
The aube and the crepuscule.

So, when I weary of praising the dawn and the sunset,
Let me be no more counted among the immortals;
But number me amid the wearying ones,
Let me be a man as the herd,
And as the slave that is given in barter.

CHRISTOPHORI COLUMBI TUMULUS

(From the Latin of Hippolytus Capilupus, Early Cent. MDC)

Genoan, glory of Italy, Columbus thou sure light,
Alas the urn takes even thee so soon out-blown,
Its little space

Doth hold thee, whom Oceanus had not the might
Within his folds to hold, altho' his broad embrace
Doth hold all lands.

Bark-borne beyond his boundries unto Hind thou wast
Where scarce Fame's volant self the way had cast.

HISTRION

No man hath dared to write this thing as yet,
And yet I know, how that the souls of all men great
At times pass through us,
And we are melted into them, and are not
Save reflexions of their souls.
Thus am I Dante for a space and am
One François Villon, ballad-lord and thief
Or am such holy ones I may not write,
Lest blasphemy be writ against my name;
This for an instant and the flame is gone.

'Tis as in midmost us there glows a sphere
Translucent, molten gold, that is the "I"
And into this some form projects itself:
Christus, or John, or eke the Florentine;
And as the clear space is not if a form's
Imposed thereon,
So cease we from all being for the time,
And these, the Masters of the Soul, live on.

71

NEL BIANCHEGGIAR

Blue-grey, and white, and white-of-rose,
The flowers of the West's fore-dawn unclose.
I feel the dusky softness whirr
of color, as upon a dulcimer
"Her" dreaming fingers lay between the tunes,
As when the living music swoons
But dies not quite, because for love of us
—knowing our state
How that 'tis troublous—
It wills not die to leave us desolate.

With thanks to Marco Londonio for his delightful Italian paraphrase of these lines appearing in "La Bauta" for Aug. 9th.

TO T. H.   THE AMPHORA.

Bring me this day some poet of the past,
Some unknown shape amid the wonder lords!
Yea of such wine as all time's store affords
From rich amphorae that nor years can blast
With might of theirs and blows down-rainèd fast,
Falernian and Massic of the Roman hoards,
I've drunk the best that any land accords,
Yet dread the time that I shall drink the last.

Bring me this day from out the smoky room
Some curved clay guardian of untasted wine,
That holds the sun at heart. Search i' the gloom
Boy, well, and mark you that the draught be good.
Then as an answer to this jest of mine,
Luck brought th' amphora, and the clasp was "Hood."

PERSONAE

1909

First published in April, 1909

PERSONAE

OF

EZRA POUND

LONDON

ELKIN MATHEWS, VIGO STREET

MCMIX

Title page of Personae, *London, 1909*

THIS BOOK IS FOR

MARY MOORE

OF TRENTON, IF SHE

WANTS IT

PRAISE OF YSOLT

In vain have I striven
      to teach my heart to bow;
In vain have I said to him
"There be many singers greater than thou."

But his answer cometh, as winds and as lutany,
As a vague crying upon the night
That leaveth me no rest, saying ever,
              "Song, a song."

Their echoes play upon each other in the twilight
Seeking ever a song.
Lo, I am worn with travail
And the wandering of many roads hath made my eyes
As dark red circles filled with dust.
Yet there is a trembling upon me in the twilight,
      And little red elf words   crying "A song,"
      Little grey elf words   crying for a song,
      Little brown leaf words   crying "A song,"
      Little green leaf words   crying for a song.
The words are as leaves, old brown leaves in the
      spring time
Blowing they know not whither, seeking a song.

White words as snow flakes but they are cold
Moss words, lip words, words of slow streams.

In vain have I striven
      to teach my soul to bow,
In vain have I pled with him,
      "There be greater souls than thou."

For in the morn of my years there came a woman
As moon light calling
As the moon calleth the tides,
             "Song, a song."
Wherefore I made her a song and she went from me

As the moon doth from the sea,
But still came the leaf words, little brown elf words
Saying "The soul sendeth us."
                    "A song, a song!"
And in vain I cried unto them "I have no song
For she I sang of hath gone from me."

But my soul sent a woman, a woman of the wonderfolk,
A woman as fire upon the pine woods
        crying "Song, a song."
As the flame crieth unto the sap.
My song was ablaze with her and she went from me
As flame leaveth the embers so went she unto new
        forests
And the words were with me
        crying ever "Song, a song."

And I "I have no song,"
Till my soul sent a woman as the sun:
Yea as the sun calleth to the seed,
As the spring upon the bough
So is she that cometh the song- drawer
She that holdeth the wonder words within her eyes
The words little elf words
        that call ever unto me
                    "Song, a song."

ENVOI

In vain have I striven with my soul
        to teach my soul to bow.
What soul boweth
        while in his heart art thou?

TALLY-O

What ho! the wind is up and eloquent.
Through all the Winter's halls he crieth Spring.
Now will I get me up unto mine own forests
And behold their bourgeoning.

AT THE HEART O' ME

A.D. 751

With ever one fear at the heart o' me
Long by still sea-coasts
    coursed my Grey-Falcon,
And the twin delights
    of shore and sea were mine,
Sapphire and emerald with
    fine pearls between.

Through the pale courses of
    the land-caressing in-streams
Glided my barge and
    the kindly strange peoples
Gave to me laugh for laugh,
    and wine for my tales of wandering.
And the cities gave me welcome
    and the fields free passage,
With ever one fear
    at the heart o' me.

An thou should'st grow weary
    ere my returning,
An *"they"* should call to thee
    from out the borderland,

What should avail me
    booty of whale-ways?
What should avail me
    gold rings or the chain-mail?
What should avail me
    the many-twined bracelets?
What should avail me,
    O my beloved,
Here in this "Middan-gard" *
    what should avail me
Out of the booty and
    gain of my goings?

XENIA

And
Unto thine eyes my heart
Sendeth old dreams of the spring-time,
Yea of wood-ways my rime
Found thee and flowers in and of all streams
That sang low burthen, and of roses,
That lost their dew-bowed petals for the dreams
We scattered o'er them passing by.

OCCIDIT

Autumnal breaks the flame upon the sun-set herds.
The sheep on Gilead as tawn hair gleam
Neath Mithra's dower and his slow departing,
While in the sky a thousand fleece of gold
Bear, each his tribute, to the waning god.

* Anglo-Saxon, "Earth."

Hung on the rafters of the effulgent west,
Their tufted splendour shields his decadence,
As in our southern lands brave tapestries
Are hung king-greeting from the ponticells
And drag the pageant from the earth to air,
Wherein the storied figures live again,
Wind-molden back unto their life's erst guise,
All tremulous beneath the many-fingered breath
That Aufidus * doth take to house his soul.

AN IDYL FOR GLAUCUS

> *Nel suo aspetto tal dentro mi fei*
> *Qual si fe' Glauco nel gustar dell' erba*
> *Che il fe' consorto in mar degli altri dei.*
> Paradiso, 1, 67-9.

"As Glaucus tasting the grass that made
him sea-fellow with the other gods."

I

Whither he went I may not follow him. His eyes
Were strange to-day. They always were,
After their fashion, kindred of the sea.

To-day I found him. It is very long
That I had sought among the nets, and when I asked
The fishermen, they laughed at me.
I sought long days amid the cliffs thinking to find
The body-house of him, and then
There at the blue cave-mouth my joy
Grew pain for suddenness, to see him 'live.
Whither he went I may not come, it seems
He is become estranged from all the rest,
And all the sea is now his wonder-house.

* The West Wind.

And he may sink unto strange depths, he tells me of,
That have no light as we it deem.
E'en now he speaks strange words. I did not know
One half the substance of his speech with me.

And then when I saw naught he sudden leaped
And shot, a gleam of silver, down, away.
And I have spent three days upon this rock
And yet he comes no more.
He did not even seem to know
I watched him gliding through the vitreous deep.

II

They chide me that the skein I used to spin
Holds not my interest now,
They mock me at the route, well, I have come again.
Last night I saw three white forms move
Out past the utmost wave that bears the white foam crest.
I somehow knew that he was one of them.

Oimè, Oimè! I think each time they come
Up from the sea heart to the realm of air
They are more far-removèd from the shore.
When first I found him here, he slept
E'en as he might after a long night's taking on the deep.
And when he woke some whit the old kind smile
Dwelt round his lips and held him near to me.
But then strange gleams shot through the grey-deep eyes
As though he saw beyond and saw not me.
And when he moved to speak it troubled him.
And then he plucked at grass and bade me eat.
And then forgot me for the sea its charm
And leapt him in the wave and so was gone.

III

I wonder why he mocked me with the grass.
I know not any more how long it is
Since I have dwelt not in my mother's house.
I know they think me mad, for all night long
I haunt the sea-marge, thinking I may find

Some day the herb he offered unto me.
Perhaps he did not jest; they say some simples have
More wide-spanned power than old wives draw from them.
Perhaps, found I this grass, he'd come again.
Perhaps 'tis some strange charm to draw him here,
'Thout which he may not leave his new-found crew
That ride the two-foot coursers of the deep,
And laugh in storms and break the fishers' nets.
Oimè, Oimè!

SONG
Voices in the Wind.

We have worn the blue and vair,
And all the sea-caves
Know us of old, and know our new-found mate.
There's many a secret stair
The sea-folk climb . . .

Out of the Wind.
Oimè, Oimè!

I wonder why the wind, even the wind doth seem
To mock me now, all night, all night, and
Have I strayed among the cliffs here.
They say, some day I'll fall
Down through the sea-bit fissures, and no more
Know the warm cloak of sun, or bathe
The dew across my tired eyes to comfort them.
They try to keep me hid within four walls.
I will not stay!
            Oimè!
And the wind saith; Oimè!

I am quite tired now. I know the grass
Must grow somewhere along this Thracian coast,
If only he would come some little while and find it me.

ENDETH THE LAMENT FOR GLAUCUS

IN DURANCE

I am homesick after mine own kind,
Oh I know that there are folk about me, friendly faces,
But I am homesick after mine own kind.

"These sell our pictures"! Oh well,
They reach me not, touch me some edge or that,
But reach me not and all my life's become
One flame, that reacheth not beyond
Mine heart's own hearth,
Or hides among the ashes there for thee.
"Thee"? Oh "thee" is who cometh first
Out of mine own soul-kin,
For I am homesick after mine own kind
And ordinary people touch me not.
                              Yea, I am homesick
After mine own kind that know, and feel
And have some breath for beauty and the arts.

Aye, I am wistful for my kin of the spirit
And have none about me save in the shadows
When come *they*, surging of power, "DAEMON,"
"Quasi KALOUN." S.T. says, Beauty is most that, a
      "calling to the soul."
Well then, so call they, the swirlers out of the mist
      of my soul,
They that come mewards bearing old magic.

But for all that, I am homesick after mine own kind
And would meet kindred e'en as I am,
Flesh-shrouded bearing the secret.
"All they that with strange sadness"
Have the earth in mock'ry, and are kind to all,
My fellows, aye I know the glory
Of th' unbounded ones, but ye, that hide
As I hide most the while
And burst forth to the windows only whiles or whiles
For love, or hope, or beauty or for power,

Then smoulder, with the lids half closed
And are untouched by echoes of the world.

Oh ye, my fellows: with the seas between us some be,
Purple and sapphire for the silver shafts
Of sun and spray all shattered at the bows
Of such a "Veltro" of the vasty deep
As bore my tortoise house scant years agone:
And some the hills hold off,
The little hills to east us, though here we
Have damp and plain to be our shutting in.

And yet my soul sings "Up!" and we are one.
Yea thou, and Thou, and THOU, and all my kin
To whom my breast and arms are ever warm,
For that I love ye as the wind the trees
That holds their blossoms and their leaves in cure
And calls the utmost singing from the boughs
That 'thout him, save the aspen, were as dumb
Still shade, and bade no whisper speak the birds of how
"Beyond, beyond, beyond, there lies . . ."

GUILLAUME DE LORRIS BELATED

A Vision of Italy

Wisdom set apart from all desire,
A hoary Nestor with youth's own glad eyes,
Him met I at the style, and all benign
He greeted me an equal and I knew,
By this his lack of pomp, he was himself.

Slow-Smiling is companion unto him,
And Mellow-Laughter serves, his trencherman.
And I a thousand beauties there beheld.
And he and they made merry endlessly.

And love was rayed between them as a mist,
And yet so fine and delicate a haze
It did impede the eyes no whit,
Unless it were to make the halo round each one
Appear more myriad-jewelled marvellous,
Than any pearled and ruby diadem the courts o' earth
     ha' known.

Slender as mist-wrought maids and hamadryads
Did meseem these shapes that ministered,
These formed harmonies with lake-deep eyes,
And first the cities of north Italy
I did behold,
Each as a woman wonder-fair,
And svelte Verona first I met at eve;
And in the dark we kissed and then the way
Bore us somewhile apart.
And yet my heart keeps tryst with her,
So every year our thoughts are interwove
As fingers were, such times as eyes see much, and tell.
And she that loved the master years agone,
That bears his signet in her "Signor Square,"
"Che lo glorifico." [1]
               She spread her arms,
And in that deep embrace
All thoughts of woe were perished
And of pain and weariness and all the wrack
Of light-contending thoughts and battled-gleams,
(That our intelligence doth gain by strife against itself)
Of things we have not yet the earnèd right to clearly see.
And all, yea all that dust doth symbolize
Was there forgot, and my enfranchised soul
Grew as the liquid elements, and was infused
With joy that is not light, nor might nor harmony,
And yet hath part and quality of all these three,
Whereto is added calm past earthly peace.

Thus with Verona's spirit, and all time
Swept on beyond my ken, and as the sea

Hath in no wise a form within itself,
Cioè, as liquid hath no form save where it bounden is
By some enshrouding chalice of hard things—
As wine its graven goblet, and the sea
Its wave-hewn basalt for a bordering,
So had my thought and now my thought's remembrance
No "*in*formation" of whatso there passed
For this long space the dream-king's horny gate.

And when that age was done and the transfusion
Of all my self through her and she through me,
I did perceive that she enthroned two things:
Verona, and a maid I knew on earth;
And dulled some while from dream, and then become
That lower thing, deductive intellect, I saw
How all things are but symbols of all things,[2]
And each of many, do we know
But the equation governing.
And in my rapture at this vision's scope
I saw no end or bourn to what things mean,
So praised Pythagoras and once more raised
By this said rapture to the house of Dream,
Beheld Fenicè as a lotus-flower
Drift through the purple of the wedded sea
And grow a wraith and then a dark-eyed she,
And knew her name was "All-forgetfulness,"
And hailed her: "Princess of the Opiates,"
And guessed her evil and her good thereby.

And then a maid of nine "Pavia" hight,
Passed with a laugh that was all mystery,
And when I turned to her
She reached me one clear chalice of white wine,
Pressed from the recent grapes that yet were hung
Adown her shoulders, and were bound
Right cunningly about her elfish brows;
So hale a draught, the life of every grape
Lurked without ferment in the amber cloud.
And memory, this wine was, of all good.

And more I might have seen: Firenza, Goito,
Or that proudest gate, Ligurian Genoa,
Cornelia of Colombo of far sight,
That, man and seer in one, had well been twain,
And each a glory to his hills and sea;
And past her a great band
Bright garlanded or rich with purple skeins,
And crimson mantles and queynt fineries
That tarnished held but so the more
Of dim allurement in their half-shown folds:
So swept my vision o'er their filmy ranks,
Then rose some opaque cloud,
Whose name I have not yet discerned,
And music as I heard it one clear night
Within our earthly night's own mirroring,
Cioè, San?————San Pietro by Adige,[3]
Where altar candles blazed out as dim stars,
And all the gloom was soft, and shadowy forms
Made and sang God, within the far-off choir.
And in a clear space high behind
Them and the tabernacle of that place,
Two tapers shew the master of the keys
As some white power pouring forth itself.

And all the church rang low and murmured
Thus in my dream of forms the music swayed.
And I was lost in it and only woke
When something like a mass bell rang, and then
That white-foot wind, pale Dawn's annunciatrice,
Me bore to earth again, but some strange peace
I had not known so well before this swevyn
Clung round my head and made me hate earth less.

For notes on this poem see end of volume.

IN THE OLD AGE OF THE SOUL

I do not choose to dream; there cometh on me
Some strange old lust for deeds.
As to the nerveless hand of some old warrior
The sword-hilt or the war-worn wonted helmet
Brings momentary life and long-fled cunning,
So to my soul grown old—
Grown old with many a jousting, many a foray,
Grown old with many a hither-coming and hence-going—
Till now they send him dreams and no more deed;
So doth he flame again with might for action,
Forgetful of the council of the elders,
Forgetful that who rules doth no more battle,
Forgetful that such might no more cleaves to him
So doth he flame again toward valiant doing.

ALBA BELINGALIS

Phoebus shineth ere his splendour flieth
Aurora drives faint light athwart the land
And the drowsy watcher crieth,
                              "ARISE."

            Ref.
O'er cliff and ocean the white dawn appeareth
It passeth vigil and the shadows cleareth.

They be careless of the gates, delaying,
Whom the ambush glides to hinder,
Whom I warn and cry to, praying,
                              "ARISE."

            Ref.
O'er cliff and ocean the white dawn appeareth
It passeth vigil and the shadows cleareth.

Forth from out Arcturus, North Wind bloweth
The stars of heaven sheathe their glory
And sun-driven forth-goeth
                              Settentrion.

Ref.

O'er sea mist, and mountain is the dawn display'd
It passeth watch and maketh night afraid.

From a tenth-century ms.

FROM SYRIA

> The song of Peire Bremon "Lo Tort" that he made for his
> Lady in Provença: he being in Syria a crusader.

In April when I see all through
Mead and garden new flowers blow,
And streams with ice-bands broken flow,
Eke hear the birds their singing do;
When spring's grass-perfume floateth by
Then 'tis sweet song and birdlet's cry
Do make mine old joy come anew.

Such time was wont my thought of old
To wander in the ways of love.
Burnishing arms and clang thereof,
And honour-services manifold
Be now my need. Whoso combine
Such works, love is his bread and wine,
Wherefore should his fight the more be bold.

Song bear I, who tears should bring
Sith ire of love mak'th me annoy,
With song think I to make me joy.
Yet ne'er have I heard said this thing:

"He sings who sorrow's guise should wear."
Natheless I will not despair
That sometime I'll have cause to sing.

I should not to despair give way
That somewhile I'll my lady see.
I trust well He that lowered me
Hath power again to make me gay.
But if e'er I come to my Love's land
And turn again to Syrian strand,
God keep me there for a fool, alway!

God for a miracle well should
Hold my coming from her away,
And hold me in His grace alway
That I left her, for holy-rood.
An I lose her, no joy for me,
Pardi, hath the wide world in fee.
Nor could He mend it, if He would.

Well did she know sweet wiles to take
My heart, when thence I took my way.
'Thout sighing, pass I ne'er a day
For that sweet semblance she did make
To me, saying all in sorrow:
"Sweet friend, and what of me to-morrow?"
"Love mine, why wilt me so forsake?"

ENVOI

Beyond sea be thou sped, my song,
And, by God, to my Lady say
That in desirous, grief-filled way
My nights and my days are full long.
And command thou William the Long-Seer
To tell thee to my Lady dear,
That comfort be her thoughts among.

The only bit of Peire Bremon's work that has come down to us, and through its being printed with the songs of Giraut of Bornelh he is like to lose credit for even this.—E.P.

FROM THE SADDLE

D'Aubigné to Diane

Wearied by wind and wave death goes
With gin and snare right near alway
Unto my sight. Behind me bay
As hounds the tempests of my foes.
Ever on ward against such woes,
Pistols my pillow's service pay,
Yet Love makes me the poet play.
Thou know'st the rime demands repose,
So if my line disclose distress,
The soldier and my restlessness
And teen, Pardon, dear Lady mine,
For since mid war I bear love's pain
'Tis meet my verse, as I, show sign
Of powder, gun-match and sulphur stain.

MARVOIL

A poor clerk I, "Arnaut the less" they call me,
And because I have small mind to sit
Day long, long day cooped on a stool
A-jumbling o' figures for Maitre Jacques Polin,
I ha' taken to rambling the South here.

The Vicomte of Beziers's not such a bad lot.
I made rimes to his lady this three year:
Vers and canzone, till that damn'd son of Aragon,
Alfonso the half-bald, took to hanging
His helmet at Beziers.
Then came what might come, to wit: three men and
    one woman,

Beziers off at Mont-Ausier, I and his lady
Singing the stars in the turrets of Beziers,
And one lean Aragonese cursing the seneschal
To the end that you see, friends:

Aragon cursing in Aragon, Beziers busy at Beziers—
Bored to an inch of extinction,
Tibors all tongue and temper at Mont-Ausier,
Me! in this damn'd inn of Avignon,
Stringing long verse for the Burlatz;
All for one half-bald, knock-knee'd king of the
        Aragonese,
Alfonso, Quatro, poke-nose.

And if when I am dead
They take the trouble to tear out this wall here,
They'll know more of Arnaut of Marvoil
Than half his canzoni say of him.
As for will and testament I leave none,
Save this: "Vers and canzone to the Countess
        of Beziers
In return for the first kiss she gave me."
May her eyes and her cheek be fair
To all men except the King of Aragon,
And may I come speedily to Beziers
Whither my desire and my dream have preceded me.

O hole in the wall here! be thou my jongleur
As ne'er had I other, and when the wind blows,
Sing thou the grace of the Lady of Beziers,
For even as thou art hollow before I fill thee with
        this parchment,
So is my heart hollow when she filleth not mine eyes,
And so were my mind hollow, did she not fill utterly
        my thought.

Wherefore, O hole in the wall here,
When the wind blows sigh thou for my sorrow
That I have not the Countess of Beziers

Close in my arms here.
Even as thou shalt soon have this parchment.

O hole in the wall here, be thou my jongleur,
And though thou sighest my sorrow in the wind,
Keep yet my secret in thy breast here;
Even as I keep her image in my heart here.

Mihi pergamena deest.

REVOLT

Against the Crepuscular Spirit in Modern Poetry

I would shake off the lethargy of this our time,
        and give
For shadows—shapes of power
For dreams—men.

"It is better to dream than do"?
                Aye! and, No!

Aye! if we dream great deeds, strong men,
Hearts hot, thoughts mighty.

No! if we dream pale flowers,
Slow-moving pageantry of hours that languidly
Drop as o'er-ripened fruit from sallow trees.
If so we live and die not life but dreams,
Great God, grant life in dreams,
Not dalliance, but life!

Let us be men that dream,
Not cowards, dabblers, waiters
For dead Time to reawaken and grant balm
For ills unnamed.

Great God, if we be damn'd to be not men but only dreams,
Then let us be such dreams the world shall tremble at
And know we be its rulers though but dreams!
Then let us be such shadows as the world shall tremble at
And know we be its masters though but shadow!

Great God, if men are grown but pale sick phantoms
That must live only in these mists and tempered lights
And tremble for dim hours that knock o'er loud
Or tread too violent in passing them;

Great God, if these thy sons are grown such thin ephemera,
I bid thee grapple chaos and beget
Some new titanic spawn to pile the hills and stir
This earth again.

AND THUS IN NINEVEH

"Aye! I am a poet and upon my tomb
Shall maidens scatter rose leaves
And men myrtles, ere the night
Slays day with her dark sword.

"Lo! this thing is not mine
Nor thine to hinder,
For the custom is full old,
And here in Nineveh have I beheld
Many a singer pass and take his place
In those dim halls where no man troubleth
His sleep or song.
And many a one hath sung his songs
More craftily, more subtle-souled than I;
And many a one now doth surpass
My wave-worn beauty with his wind of flowers,
Yet am I poet, and upon my tomb
Shall all men scatter rose leaves

Ere the night slay light
With her blue sword.

"It is not, Raama, that my song rings highest
Or more sweet in tone than any, but that I
Am here a Poet, that doth drink of life
As lesser men drink wine."

THE WHITE STAG

I ha' seen them 'mid the clouds on the heather.
Lo! they pause not for love nor for sorrow,
Yet their eyes are as the eyes of a maid to her lover,
When the white hart breaks his cover
And the white wind breaks the morn.

> " 'Tis the white stag, Fame, we're a-hunting,
> Bid the world's hounds come to horn!"

Piccadilly

Beautiful, tragical faces,
Ye that were whole, and are so sunken;
And, O ye vile, ye that might have been loved,
That are so sodden and drunken,
> *Who hath forgotten you?*

O wistful, fragile faces, few out of many!

The gross, the coarse, the brazen,
God knows I cannot pity them, perhaps, as I should do,
But, oh, ye delicate, wistful faces,
> *Who hath forgotten you?*

NOTES ON NEW POEMS

1. *"che lo glorifico."* In the Piazza dei Signori, you will find an inscription which translates thus:

"It is here Can Grande della Scala gave welcome to Dante Alighieri, the *same which glorified him,* dedicating to him that third his song eternal."

> "C.G. vi accolse D. A. che lo
> glorifico dedicandogli la terza,
> delle eterne sue cantiche."

2. Ref. Richard of St. Victor. "On the preparation of the soul for contemplation," where he distinguishes between cogitation, meditation, and contemplation.

In cogitation the thought or attention flits aimlessly about the subject.

In meditation it circles round it, that is, it views it systematically, from all sides, gaining perspective.

In contemplation it radiates from a centre, that is, as light from the sun it reaches out in an infinite number of ways to things that are related to or dependent on it.

The words above are my own, as I have not the Benjamin Minor by me.

Following St. Victor's figure of radiation: Poetry in its acme is expression from contemplation.

3. San Pietro Incarnato. There are several rows of houses intervening between it and the river.

ALBA BELINGALIS

MS. in Latin, with refrain,

> "L alba par umet mar atras el poy
> Pas abigil miraclar Tenebris."

It was and may still be the oldest fragment of Provençal known.

The Personae are:

Arnaut of Marvoil, a troubadour, date 1170–1200.

The Countess (in her own right) of Burlatz, and of Beziers, being the wife of

The Vicomte of Beziers.

Alfonso IV of Aragon.

Tibors of Mont-Ausier. For fuller mention of her see the "razos" on Bertran of Born. She is contemporary with the other persons, but I have no strict warrant for dragging her name into this particular affair.

Marco Londonio's Italian version of "Nel Biancheggiar":

Nel biancheggiar di delicata rosa
Risplendono i colori
D' occidentali fiori
Prima che l'alba, in esultanza ascosa

Voglia baciarli. Ed aleggiar io sento
Qual su dolce lïuto
Nel lor linguaggio muto
Fiorir di gioia e tocco di tormento

Cosi un' arcano senso di languore,
Le sue sognanti dita
Fanno scordar la vita
Spirando in verso tutto pien d'amore . . .

Senza morir: chè sanno i suoni alati,
Vedendo il nostro stato,
Ch' è dal dolor turbato,
Di lasciarci, morendo, desolati.

EXULTATIONS

1909

EXULTATIONS

OF

EZRA POUND

LONDON

ELKIN MATHEWS, VIGO STREET

M CM IX

Title page of Exultations, *London, 1909*

I am an eternal spirit and the things I make are but ephemera, yet I endure:

Yea, and the little earth crumbles beneath our feet and we endure.

GUIDO INVITES YOU THUS *

"Lappo I leave behind and Dante too,
Lo, I would sail the seas with thee alone!
Talk me no love talk, no bought-cheap fiddl'ry,
Mine is the ship and thine the merchandise,
All the blind earth knows not th' emprise
Whereto thou calledst and whereto I call.

Lo, I have seen thee bound about with dreams,
Lo, I have known thy heart and its desire;
Life, all of it, my sea, and all men's streams
Are fused in it as flames of an altar fire!

Lo, thou hast voyaged not! The ship is mine."

* The reference is to Dante's sonnet "Guido vorrei . . ."

SESTINA: ALTAFORTE

Loquitur: *En* Bertrans de Born.
    Dante Alighieri put this man in hell for that he was a
    stirrer-up of strife.
    Eccovi!
    Judge ye!
    Have I dug him up again?
The scene is at his castle, Altaforte. "Papiols" is his jongleur.
"The Leopard," the *device* of Richard (Cœur de Lion).

I

Damn it all! all this our South stinks peace.
You whoreson dog, Papiols, come! Let's to music!
I have no life save when the swords clash.
But ah! when I see the standards gold, vair, purple, opposing
And the broad fields beneath them turn crimson,
Then howl I my heart nigh mad with rejoicing.

II

In hot summer have I great rejoicing
When the tempests kill the earth's foul peace,
And the light'nings from black heav'n flash crimson,
And the fierce thunders roar me their music
And the winds shriek through the clouds mad, opposing,
And through all the riven skies God's swords clash.

III

Hell grant soon we hear again the swords clash!
And the shrill neighs of destriers in battle rejoicing,
Spiked breast to spiked breast opposing!
Better one hour's stour than a year's peace
With fat boards, bawds, wine and frail music!
Bah! there's no wine like the blood's crimson!

IV

And I love to see the sun rise blood-crimson.
And I watch his spears through the dark clash
And it fills all my heart with rejoicing
And pries wide my mouth with fast music

When I see him so scorn and defy peace,
His lone might 'gainst all darkness opposing.

V

The man who fears war and squats opposing
My words for stour, hath no blood of crimson
But is fit only to rot in womanish peace
Far from where worth's won and the swords clash
For the death of such sluts I go rejoicing;
Yea, I fill all the air with my music.

VI

Papiols, Papiols, to the music!
There's no sound like to swords swords opposing,
No cry like the battle's rejoicing
When our elbows and swords drip the crimson
And our charges 'gainst "The Leopard's" rush clash.
May God damn for ever all who cry "Peace!"

VII

And let the music of the swords make them crimson!
Hell grant soon we hear again the swords clash!
Hell blot black for alway the thought "Peace"!

PIERE VIDAL OLD

It is of Piere Vidal, the fool par excellence of all Provence,
of whom the tale tells how he ran mad, as a wolf, because of
his love for Loba of Penautier, and how men hunted him
with dogs through the mountains of Cabaret and brought him
for dead to the dwelling of this Loba (she-wolf) of Penautier,
and how she and her Lord had him healed and made welcome,
and he stayed some time at that court. He speaks:

When I but think upon the great dead days
And turn my mind upon that splendid madness,
Lo! I do curse my strength

And blame the sun his gladness;
For that the one is dead
And the red sun mocks my sadness.

Behold me, Vidal, that was fool of fools!
Swift as the king wolf was I and as strong
When tall stags fled me through the alder brakes,
And every jongleur knew me in his song,
And the hounds fled and the deer fled
And none fled over long.

Even the grey pack knew me and knew fear.
God! how the swiftest hind's blood spurted hot
Over the sharpened teeth and purpling lips!
Hot was that hind's blood yet it scorched me not
As did first scorn, then lips of the Penautier!
Aye ye are fools, if ye think time can blot

From Piere Vidal's remembrance that blue night.
God! but the purple of the sky was deep!
Clear, deep, translucent, so the stars me seemed
Set deep in crystal; and because my sleep
—Rare visitor—came not,—the Saints I guerdon
For that restlessness—Piere set to keep

One more fool's vigil with the hollyhocks.
Swift came the Loba, as a branch that's caught,
Torn, green and silent in the swollen Rhone,
Green was her mantle, close, and wrought
Of some thin silk stuff that's scarce stuff at all,
But like a mist wherethrough her white form fought,

And conquered! Ah God! conquered!
Silent my mate came as the night was still.
Speech? Words? Faugh! Who talks of words
        and love?!
Hot is such love and silent,
Silent as fate is, and as strong until
It faints in taking and in giving all.

Stark, keen, triumphant, till it plays at death.
God! she was white then, splendid as some tomb
High wrought of marble, and the panting breath
Ceased utterly. Well, then I waited, drew,
Half-sheathed, then naked from its saffron sheath
Drew full this dagger that doth tremble here.

Just then she woke and mocked the less keen blade.
Ah God, the Loba! and my only mate!
Was there such flesh made ever and unmade!
God curse the years that turn such women grey!
Behold here Vidal, that was hunted, flayed,
Shamed and yet bowed not and that won at last.

And yet I curse the sun for his red gladness,
I that have known strath, garth, brake, dale,
And every run-way of the wood through that great
        madness,
Behold me shrivelled as an old oak's trunk
And made men's mock'ry in my rotten sadness!

No man hath heard the glory of my days:
No man hath dared and won his dare as I:
One night, one body and one welding flame!
What do ye own, ye niggards! that can buy
Such glory of the earth? Or who will win
Such battle-guerdon with his "prowesse high"?

O Age gone lax! O stunted followers,
That mask at passions and desire desires,
Behold me shrivelled, and your mock of mocks;
And yet I mock you by the mighty fires
That burnt me to this ash.

. . . .

Ah! Cabaret! Ah Cabaret, thy hills again!

. . . .

Take your hands off me! . . .   [*Sniffing the air.*
                        Ha! this scent is hot!

BALLAD OF THE GOODLY FERE *

Simon Zelotes speaketh it somewhile after the Crucifixion.

Ha' we lost the goodliest fere o' all
For the priests and the gallows tree?
Aye lover he was of brawny men,
O' ships and the open sea.

When they came wi' a host to take Our Man
His smile was good to see,
"First let these go!" quo' our Goodly Fere,
"Or I'll see ye damned," says he.

Aye he sent us out through the crossed high spears
And the scorn of his laugh rang free,
"Why took ye not me when I walked about
Alone in the town?" says he.

Oh we drank his "Hale" in the good red wine
When we last made company,
No capon priest was the Goodly Fere
But a man o' men was he.

I ha' seen him drive a hundred men
Wi' a bundle o' cords swung free,
That they took the high and holy house
For their pawn and treasury.

They'll no' get him a' in a book I think
Though they write it cunningly;
No mouse of the scrolls was the Goodly Fere
But aye loved the open sea.

If they think they ha' snared our Goodly Fere
They are fools to the last degree.
"I'll go to the feast," quo' our Goodly Fere,
"Though I go to the gallows tree."

* Fere = Mate, Companion.

"Ye ha' seen me heal the lame and blind,
And wake the dead," says he,
"Ye shall see one thing to master all:
'Tis how a brave man dies on the tree."

A son of God was the Goodly Fere
That bade us his brothers be.
I ha' seen him cow a thousand men.
I have seen him upon the tree.

He cried no cry when they drave the nails
And the blood gushed hot and free,
The hounds of the crimson sky gave tongue
But never a cry cried he.

I ha' seen him cow a thousand men
On the hills o' Galilee,
They whined as he walked out calm between,
Wi' his eyes like the grey o' the sea.

Like the sea that brooks no voyaging
With the winds unleashed and free,
Like the sea that he cowed at Genseret
Wi' twey words spoke' suddently.

A master of men was the Goodly Fere,
A mate of the wind and sea,
If they think they ha' slain our Goodly Fere
They are fools eternally.

I ha' seen him eat o' the honey-comb
Sin' they nailed him to the tree.

HYMN III

From the Latin of Marc Antony Flaminius, sixteenth century

As a fragile and lovely flower unfolds its gleaming
      foliage on the breast of the fostering earth, if
      the dew and the rain draw it forth;
So doth my tender mind flourish, if it be fed with the
      sweet dew of the fostering spirit,
Lacking this, it beginneth straightway to languish,
      even as a floweret born upon dry earth, if the
      dew and the rain tend it not.

SESTINA FOR YSOLT

There comes upon me will to speak in praise
Of things most fragile in their loveliness;
Because the sky hath wept all this long day
And wrapped men's hearts within its cloak of greyness,
Because they look not down I sing the stars,
Because 'tis still mid-March I praise May's flowers.

Also I praise long hands that lie as flowers
Which though they labour not are worthy praise,
And praise deep eyes like pools wherein the stars
Gleam out reflected in their loveliness,
For whoso look on such there is no greyness
May hang about his heart on any day.

The other things that I would praise to-day?
Besides white hands and all the fragile flowers,
And by their praise dispel the evening's greyness?
I praise dim hair that worthiest is of praise
And dream upon its unbound loveliness,
And how therethrough mine eyes have seen the stars.

114

Yea, through that cloud mine eyes have seen the stars
That drift out slowly when night steals the day,
Through such a cloud meseems their loveliness
Surpasses that of all the other flowers.
For that one night I give all nights my praise
And love therefrom the twilight's coming greyness.

There is a stillness in this twilight greyness
Although the rain hath veiled the flow'ry stars,
They seem to listen as I weave this praise
Of what I have not seen all this grey day,
And they will tell my praise unto the flowers
When May shall bid them in in loveliness.

O ye I love, who hold this loveliness
Near to your hearts, may never any greyness
Enshroud your hearts when ye would gather flowers,
Or bind your eyes when ye would see the stars;
But alway do I give ye flowers by day,
And when day's plucked I give ye stars for praise.

But most, thou Flower, whose eyes are like the stars,
With whom my dreams bide all the live-long day,
Within thy hands would I rest all my praise.

PORTRAIT

From "La Mère Inconnue"

Now would I weave her portrait out of all dim splendour.
Of Provence and far halls of memory,
Lo, there come echoes, faint diversity
Of blended bells at even's end, or
As the distant seas should send her
The tribute of their trembling, ceaselessly

Resonant. Out of all dreams that be,
Say, shall I bid the deepest dreams attend her?

Nay! For I have seen the purplest shadows stand
Always with reverent chere that looked on her,
Silence himself is grown her worshipper
And ever doth attend her in that land
Wherein she reigneth, wherefore let there stir
Naught but the softest voices, praising her.

"FAIR HELENA" BY RACKHAM

"What I love best in all the world?"

When the purple twilight is unbound,
    To watch her slow, tall grace
        and its wistful loveliness,
And to know her face
        is in the shadow there,
Just by two stars beneath that cloud—
The soft, dim cloud of her hair,
And to think my voice
        can reach to her
As but the rumour of some tree-bound stream,
Heard just beyond the forest's edge,
Until she all forgets I am,
And knows of me
Naught but my dream's felicity.

LAUDANTES DECEM PULCHRITUDINIS
JOHANNAE TEMPLI

I

When your beauty is grown old in all men's songs,
And my poor words are lost amid that throng,
Then you will know the truth of my poor words,
And mayhap dreaming of the wistful throng
That hopeless sigh your praises in their songs,
You will think kindly then of these mad words.

II

I am torn, torn with thy beauty,
O Rose of the sharpest thorn!
O Rose of the crimson beauty,
Why hast thou awakened the sleeper?
Why hast thou awakened the heart within me,
O Rose of the crimson thorn?

III

The unappeasable loveliness
          is calling to me out of the wind,
And because your name
          is written upon the ivory doors,
The wave in my heart is as a green wave, unconfined,
Tossing the white foam toward you;
And the lotus that pours
Her fragrance into the purple cup,
Is more to be gained with the foam
Than are you with these words of mine.

IV

He speaks to the moonlight concerning the Beloved.

Pale hair that the moon has shaken
Down over the dark breast of the sea,
O magic her beauty has shaken
About the heart of me;
Out of you have I woven a dream

That shall walk in the lonely vale
Betwixt the high hill and the low hill,
Until the pale stream
Of the souls of men quench and grow still.

V

Voices speaking to the sun.

Red leaf that art blown upward and out and over
The green sheaf of the world,
And through the dim forest and under
The shadowed arches and the aisles,
We, who are older than thou art,
Met and remembered when his eyes beheld her
In the garden of the peach-trees,
In the day of the blossoming.

VI

I stood on the hill of Yrma
      when the winds were a-hurrying,
With the grasses a-bending
      I followed them,
Through the brown grasses of Ahva
      unto the green of Asedon.
I have rested with the voices
      in the gardens of Ahthor,
I have lain beneath the peach-trees
      in the hour of the purple:

Because I had awaited in
      the garden of the peach-trees,
Because I had feared not
      in the forest of my mind,
Mine eyes beheld the vision of the blossom
There in the peach-gardens past Asedon.

O winds of Yrma, let her again come unto me,
Whose hair ye held unbound in the gardens of Ahthor!

VII

Because of the beautiful white shoulders and the
      rounded breasts
I can in no wise forget my beloved of the peach-trees,
And the little winds that speak when the dawn is
      unfurled
And the rose-colour in the grey oak-leaf's fold

When it first comes, and the glamour that rests
On the little streams in the evening; all of these
Call me to her, and all the loveliness in the world
Binds me to my beloved with strong chains of gold.

VIII

If the rose-petals which have fallen upon my eyes
And if the perfect faces which I see at times
When my eyes are closed—
Faces fragile, pale, yet flushed a little, like petals
      of roses:
If these things have confused my memories of her
So that I could not draw her face
Even if I had skill and the colours,
Yet because her face is so like these things
They but draw me nearer unto her in my thought
And thoughts of her come upon my mind gently,
As dew upon the petals of roses.

IX

He speaks to the rain.
O pearls that hang on your little silver chains,
The innumerable voices that are whispering
Among you as you are drawn aside by the wind,
Have brought to my mind the soft and eager speech
Of one who hath great loveliness,

Which is subtle as the beauty of the rains
That hang low in the moonshine and bring
The May softly among us, and unbind

The streams and the crimson and white flowers
     and reach
Deep down into the secret places.

x

The glamour of the soul hath come upon me,
And as the twilight comes upon the roses,
Walking silently among them,
So have the thoughts of my heart
Gone out slowly in the twilight
Toward my beloved,
Toward the crimson rose, the fairest.

AUX BELLES DE LONDRES

I am aweary with the utter and beautiful weariness
And with the ultimate wisdom and with things terrene,
I am aweary with your smiles and your laughter,
And the sun and the winds again
Reclaim their booty and the heart o' me.

FRANCESCA

You came in out of the night
And there were flowers in your hands,
Now you will come out of a confusion of people,
Out of a turmoil of speech about you.

I who have seen you amid the primal things
Was angry when they spoke your name
In ordinary places.
I would that the cool waves might flow over
    my mind,
And that the world should dry as a dead leaf,
Or as a dandelion seed-pod and be swept away,
So that I might find you again,
Alone.

NILS LYKKE

Beautiful, infinite memories
That are a-plucking at my heart,
Why will you be ever calling and a-calling,
And a-murmuring in the dark there?
And a-reaching out your long hands
Between me and my beloved?

And why will you be ever a-casting
The black shadow of your beauty
On the white face of my beloved
And a-glinting in the pools of her eyes?

A SONG OF THE VIRGIN MOTHER

In the play "Los Pastores de Belen"
From the Spanish of Lope de Vega

As ye go through these palm-trees
O holy angels;
Sith sleepeth my child here
Still ye the branches.

O Bethlehem palm-trees
That move to the anger
Of winds in their fury,
Tempestuous voices,
Make ye no clamour,
Run ye less swiftly,
Sith sleepeth the child here
Still ye your branches.

He the divine child
Is here a-wearied
Of weeping the earth-pain,
Here for his rest would he
Cease from his mourning,
Only a little while,
Sith sleepeth this child here
Stay ye the branches.

Cold be the fierce winds,
Treacherous round him.
Ye see that I have not
Wherewith to guard him,
O angels, divine ones
That pass us a-flying,
Sith sleepeth my child here
Stay ye the branches.

PLANH FOR THE YOUNG ENGLISH KING

> That is, Prince Henry Plantagenet, elder brother
> to Richard "Cœur de Lion."
> From the Provençal of Bertrans de Born "Si tuit
> li dol elh plor elh marrimen."

If all the grief and woe and bitterness,
All dolour, ill and every evil chance
That ever came upon this grieving world
Were set together they would seem but light
Against the death of the young English King.
Worth lieth riven and Youth dolorous,
The world o'ershadowed, soiled and overcast,
Void of all joy and full of ire and sadness.

Grieving and sad and full of bitterness
Are left in teen the liegemen courteous,
The joglars supple and the troubadours.
O'er much hath ta'en Sir Death that deadly warrior
In taking from them the young English King,
Who made the freest hand seem covetous.
'Las! Never was nor will be in this world
The balance for this loss in ire and sadness!

O skilful Death and full of bitterness,
Well mayst thou boast that thou the best chevalier
That any folk e'er had, hast from us taken;
Sith nothing is that unto worth pertaineth
But had its life in the young English King,
And better were it, should God grant his pleasure
That he should live than many a living dastard
That doth but wound the good with ire and sadness.

From this faint world, how full of bitterness
Love takes his way and holds his joy deceitful,
Sith no thing is but turneth unto anguish
And each to-day 'vails less than yestere'en,
Let each man visage this young English King
That was most valiant mid all worthiest men!
Gone is his body fine and amorous,
Whence have we grief, discord and deepest sadness.

Him, whom it pleased for our great bitterness
To come to earth to draw us from misventure,
Who drank of death for our salvacioun,
Him do we pray as to a Lord most righteous
And humble eke, that the young English King
He please to pardon, as true pardon is,
And bid go in with honouréd companions
There where there is no grief, nor shall be sadness.

ALBA INNOMINATA

From the Provençal

In a garden where the whitethorn spreads her leaves
My lady hath her love lain close beside her,
Till the warder cries the dawn—Ah dawn that grieves!
Ah God! Ah God! That dawn should come so soon!

"Please God that night, dear night should never cease,
Nor that my love should parted be from me,
Nor watch cry 'Dawn'—Ah dawn that slayeth peace!
Ah God! Ah God! That dawn should come so soon!

"Fair friend and sweet, thy lips! Our lips again!
Lo, in the meadow there the birds give song!
Ours be the love and Jealousy's the pain!
Ah God! Ah God! That dawn should come so soon!

"Sweet friend and fair take we our joy again
Down in the garden, where the birds are loud,
Till the warder's reed astrain
Cry God! Ah God! That dawn should come so soon!

"Of that sweet wind that comes from Far-Away
Have I drunk deep of my Belovèd's breath,
Yea! of my Love's that is so dear and gay.
Ah God! Ah God! That dawn should come so soon!"

ENVOI
Fair is this damsel and right courteous,
And many watch her beauty's gracious way.
Her heart toward love is no wise traitorous.
Ah God! Ah God! That dawn should come so soon!"

PLANH

It is of the white thoughts that he saw in the Forest.

White Poppy, heavy with dreams,
O White Poppy, who art wiser than love,
Though I am hungry for their lips
      When I see them a-hiding
And a-passing out and in through the shadows
—There in the pine wood it is,
And they are white, White Poppy,
They are white like the clouds in the forest of the sky
Ere the stars arise to their hunting.

O White Poppy, who art wiser than love,
I am come for peace, yea from the hunting
Am I come to thee for peace.
Out of a new sorrow it is,
That my hunting hath brought me.

White Poppy, heavy with dreams,
Though I am hungry for their lips
      When I see them a-hiding
And a-passing out and in through the shadows
—And it is white they are—
But if one should look at me with the old hunger in
      her eyes,
How will I be answering her eyes?
For I have followed the white folk of the forest.

Aye! It's a long hunting
And it's a deep hunger I have when I see them
      a-gliding
And a-flickering there, where the trees stand apart.

But oh, it is sorrow and sorrow
When love dies-down in the heart.

CANZONI

1911

CANZONI

OF

EZRA POUND

LONDON

ELKIN MATHEWS, VIGO STREET

MCMXI

Title page of Canzoni, *London, 1911*

"Quos ego Persephonae maxima dona feram."

PROPERTIUS

CANZON: THE YEARLY SLAIN

(Written in reply to Manning's "Korè")
"Et huiusmodi stantiae usus est fere in omnibus cantionibus suis Arnaldus Danielis et nos eum secuti sumus." Dante, *De Vulgari Eloquio*, II. 10.

I

Ah! red-leafed time hath driven out the rose
And crimson dew is fallen on the leaf
Ere ever yet the cold white wheat be sown
That hideth all earth's green and sere and red;
The Moon-flower's fallen and the branch is bare,
Holding no honey for the starry bees;
The Maiden turns to her dark lord's demesne.

II

Fairer than Enna's field when Ceres sows
The stars of hyacinth and puts off grief,
Fairer than petals on May morning blown
Through apple-orchards where the sun hath shed
His brighter petals down to make them fair;
Fairer than these the Poppy-crowned One flees,
And Joy goes weeping in her scarlet train.

III

The faint damp wind that, ere the even, blows
Piling the west with many a tawny sheaf,
Then when the last glad wavering hours are mown
Sigheth and dies because the day is sped;
This wind is like her and the listless air
Wherewith she goeth by beneath the trees,
The trees that mock her with their scarlet stain.

IV

Love that is born of Time and comes and goes!
Love that doth hold all noble hearts in fief!
As red leaves follow where the wind hath flown,
So all men follow Love when Love is dead.
O Fate of Wind! O Wind that cannot spare,

133

But drivest out the Maid, and pourest lees
Of all thy crimson on the wold again,

V

Korè my heart is, let it stand sans gloze!
Love's pain is long, and lo, love's joy is brief!
My heart erst alway sweet is bitter grown;
As crimson ruleth in the good green's stead,
So grief hath taken all mine old joy's share
And driven forth my solace and all ease
Where pleasure bows to all-usurping pain.

VI

Crimson the hearth where one last ember glows!
My heart's new winter hath no such relief,
Nor thought of Spring whose blossom he hath known
Hath turned him back where Spring is banishèd.
Barren the heart and dead the fires there,
Blow! O ye ashes, where the winds shall please,
But cry, "Love also is the Yearly Slain."

VII

Be sped, my Canzon, through the bitter air!
To him who speaketh words as fair as these,
Say that I also know the "Yearly Slain."

CANZON: THE SPEAR

I

'Tis the clear light of love I praise
That steadfast gloweth o'er deep waters,
A clarity that gleams always.
Though man's soul pass through troubled waters,

Strange ways to him are openèd.
To shore the beaten ship is sped
If only love of light give aid.

II

That fair far spear of light now lays
Its long gold shaft upon the waters.
Ah! might I pass upon its rays
To where it gleams beyond the waters,
Or might my troubled heart be fed
Upon the frail clear light there shed,
Then were my pain at last allay'd.

III

Although the clouded storm dismays
Many a heart upon these waters,
The thought of that far golden blaze
Giveth me heart upon the waters,
Thinking thereof my bark is led
To port wherein no storm I dread;
No tempest maketh me afraid.

IV

Yet when within my heart I gaze
Upon my fair beyond the waters,
Meseems my soul within me prays
To pass straightway beyond the waters.
Though I be alway banishèd
From ways and woods that she doth tread,
One thing there is that doth not fade,

V

Deep in my heart that spear-print stays,
That wound I gat beyond the waters,
Deeper with passage of the days
That pass as swift and bitter waters,
While a dull fire within my head
Moveth itself if word be said
Which hath concern with that far maid.

VI

My love is lovelier than the sprays
Of eglantine above clear waters,
Or whitest lilies that upraise
Their heads in midst of moated waters.
No poppy in the May-glad mead
Would match her quivering lips' red
If 'gainst her lips it should be laid.

VII

The light within her eyes, which slays
Base thoughts and stilleth troubled waters,
Is like the gold where sunlight plays
Upon the still o'ershadowed waters.
When anger is there minglèd
There comes a keener gleam instead,
Like flame that burns beneath thin jade.

VIII

Know by the words here minglèd
What love hath made my heart his stead,
Glowing like flame beneath thin jade.

CANZON

To be sung beneath a window

I

Heart mine, art mine, whose embraces
Clasp but wind that past thee bloweth?
E'en this air so subtly gloweth,
Guerdoned by thy sun-gold traces,
That my heart is half afraid
For the fragrance on him laid;
Even so love's might amazes!

Man's love follows many faces,
My love only one face knoweth;
Towards thee only my love floweth,
And outstrips the swift stream's paces.
Were this love well here displayed,
As flame flameth 'neath thin jade
Love should glow through these my phrases.

III

Though I've roamed through many places,
None there is that my heart troweth
Fair as that wherein fair groweth
One whose laud here interlaces
Tuneful words, that I've essayed.
Let this tune be gently played
Which my voice herward upraises.

IV

If my praise her grace effaces,
Then 'tis not my heart that showeth,
But the skilless tongue that soweth
Words unworthy of her graces.
Tongue, that hath me so betrayed,
Were my heart but here displayed,
Then were sung her fitting praises.

CANZON: OF INCENSE

I

Thy gracious ways,
          O Lady of my heart, have
O'er all my thought their golden glamour cast;
As amber torch-flames, where strange men-at-arms
Tread softly 'neath the damask shield of night,

Rise from the flowing steel in part reflected,
So on my mailed thought that with thee goeth,
Though dark the way, a golden glamour falleth.

II

The censer sways
                    And glowing coals some art have
To free what frankincense before held fast
Till all the summer of the eastern farms
Doth dim the sense, and dream up through the light,
As memory, by new-born love corrected—
With savour such as only new love knoweth—
Through swift dim ways the hidden pasts recalleth.

III

On barren days,
                    At hours when I, apart, have
Bent low in thought of the great charm thou hast,
Behold with music's many-stringed charms
The silence groweth thou. O rare delight!
The melody upon clear strings inflected
Were dull when o'er taut sense thy presence floweth,
With quivering notes' accord that never palleth.

IV

The glowing rays
                    That from the low sun dart, have
Turned gold each tower and every towering mast;
The saffron flame, that flaming nothing harms
Hides Khadeeth's pearl and all the sapphire might
Of burnished waves, before her gates collected:
The cloak of graciousness, that round thee gloweth,
Doth hide the thing thou art, as here befalleth.

V

All things worth praise
                    That unto Khadeeth's mart have
From far been brought through perils over-passed,
All santal, myrrh, and spikenard that disarms
The pard's swift anger; these would weigh but light

'Gainst thy delights, my Khadeeth! Whence protected
By naught save her great grace that in him showeth,
My song goes forth and on her mercy calleth.

VI

O censer of the thought that golden gloweth,
Be bright before her when the evening falleth.

VII

Fragrant be thou as a new field one moweth,
O song of mine that "Hers" her mercy calleth.

CANZONE: OF ANGELS

I

He that is Lord of all the realms of light
Hath unto me from His magnificence
Granted such vision as hath wrought my joy.
Moving my spirit past the last defence
That shieldeth mortal things from mightier sight,
Where freedom of the soul knows no alloy,
I saw what forms the lordly powers employ;
Three splendours, saw I, of high holiness,
From clarity to clarity ascending
Through all the roofless, tacit courts extending
In æther which such subtle light doth bless
As ne'er the candles of the stars hath wooed;
Know ye herefrom of their similitude.

II

Withdrawn within the cavern of his wings,
Grave with the joy of thoughts beneficent,
And finely wrought and durable and clear,
If so his eyes showed forth the mind's content,
So sate the first to whom remembrance clings,

Tissued like bat's wings did his wings appear,
Not of that shadowy colouring and drear,
But as thin shells, pale saffron, luminous;
Alone, unlonely, whose calm glances shed
Friend's love to strangers though no word were said,
Pensive his godly state he keepeth thus.
Not with his surfaces his power endeth,
But is as flame that from the gem extendeth.

III

My second marvel stood not in such ease,
But he, the cloudy pinioned, winged him on
Then from my sight as now from memory,
The courier aquiline, so swiftly gone!
The third most glorious of these majesties
Give aid, O sapphires of th' eternal see,
And by your light illume pure verity.
That azure feldspar hight the microcline,
Or, on its wing, the Menelaus weareth
Such subtlety of shimmering as beareth
This marvel onward through the crystalline,
A splendid calyx that about her gloweth,
Smiting the sunlight on whose ray she goeth.

IV

The diver at Sorrento from beneath
The vitreous indigo, who swiftly riseth,
By will and not by action as it seemeth,
Moves not more smoothly, and no thought surmiseth
How she takes motion from the lustrous sheath
Which, as the trace behind the swimmer, gleameth
Yet presseth back the æther where it streameth.
To her whom it adorns this sheath imparteth
The living motion from the light surrounding;
And thus my nobler parts, to grief's confounding,
Impart into my heart a peace which starteth
From one round whom a graciousness is cast
Which clingeth in the air where she hath past.

Canzon, to her whose spirit seems in sooth
Akin unto the feldspar, since it is
So clear and subtle and azure, I send thee, saying:
That since I looked upon such potencies
And glories as are here inscribed in truth,
New boldness hath o'erthrown my long delaying,
And that thy words my new-born powers obeying—
Voices at last to voice my heart's long mood—
Are come to greet her in their amplitude.

TO OUR LADY OF VICARIOUS ATONEMENT

(Ballata)

I

Who are you that the whole world's song
Is shaken out beneath your feet
Leaving you comfortless,
Who, that, as wheat
Is garnered, gather in
The blades of man's sin
And bear that sheaf?
Lady of wrong and grief,
Blameless!

II

All souls beneath the gloom
That pass with little flames,
All these till time be run
Pass one by one
As Christs to save, and die;
What wrong one sowed,
Behold, another reaps!

141

Where lips awake our joy
The sad heart sleeps
Within.

No man doth bear his sin,
But many sins
Are gathered as a cloud about man's way.

TO GUIDO CAVALCANTI

Dante and I are come to learn of thee,
Ser Guido of Florence, master of us all,
Love, who hath set his hand upon us three,
Bidding us twain upon thy glory call.
Harsh light hath rent from us the golden pall
Of that frail sleep, *His* first light seigniory,
And we are come through all the modes that fall
Unto their lot who meet him constantly.
Wherefore, by right, in this Lord's name we greet thee,
Seeing we labour at his labour daily.
Thou, who dost know what way swift words are crossed
O thou, who hast sung till none at song defeat thee,
Grant! by thy might and hers of San Michele,
Thy risen voice send flames this pentecost.

SONNET IN TENZONE

LA MENTE
"O Thou mocked heart that cowerest by the door
And durst not honour hope with welcoming,
How shall one bid thee for her honour sing,
When song would but show forth thy sorrow's store?

What things are gold and ivory unto thee?
Go forth, thou pauper fool! Are these for naught?
Is heaven in lotus leaves? What hast thou wrought,
Or brought, or sought, wherewith to pay the fee?"

IL CUORE

"If naught I give, naught do I take return.
'Ronsard me celebroit!' behold I give
The age-old, age-old fare to fairer fair
And I fare forth into more bitter air;
Though mocked I go, yet shall her beauty live
Till rimes unrime and Truth shall truth unlearn."

SONNET: CHI È QUESTA?

Who is she coming, that the roses bend
Their shameless heads to do her passing honour?
Who is she coming with a light upon her
Not born of suns that with the day's end end?
Say is it Love who hath chosen the nobler part?
Say is it Love, that was divinity,
Who hath left his godhead that his home might be
The shameless rose of her unclouded heart?
If this be Love, where hath he won such grace?
If this be Love, how is the evil wrought,
That all men write against his darkened name?
If this be Love, if this . . .
                    O mind give place!
What holy mystery e'er was noosed in thought?
Own that thou scan'st her not, nor count it shame!

BALLATA, FRAGMENT

II

Full well thou knowest, song, what grace I mean,
E'en as thou know'st the sunlight I have lost.
Thou knowest the way of it and know'st the sheen
About her brows where the rays are bound and crossed,
E'en as thou knowest joy and know'st joy's bitter cost.
Thou know'st her grace in moving,
Thou dost her skill in loving,
Thou know'st what truth she proveth,
Thou knowest the heart she moveth,
O song where grief assoneth!

CANZON: THE VISION

I

When first I saw thee 'neath the silver mist,
Ruling thy bark of painted sandal-wood,
Did any know thee? By the golden sails
That clasped the ribbands of that azure sea,
Did any know thee save my heart alone?
O ivory woman with thy bands of gold,
Answer the song my luth and I have brought thee!

II

Dream over golden dream that secret cist,
Thy heart, O heart of me, doth hold, and mood
On mood of silver, when the day's light fails,
Say who hath touched the secret heart of thee,
Or who hath known what my heart hath not known!
O slender pilot whom the mists enfold,
Answer the song my luth and I have wrought thee!

III

When new love plucks the falcon from his wrist,
And cuts the gyve and casts the scarlet hood,
Where is the heron heart whom flight avails?
O quick to prize me Love, how suddenly
From out the tumult truth has ta'en his own,
And in this vision is our past unrolled.
Lo! With a hawk of light thy love hath caught me.

IV

And I shall get no peace from eucharist,
Nor doling out strange prayers before the rood,
To match the peace that thine hands' touch entails;
Nor doth God's light match light shed over me
When thy caught sunlight is about me thrown,
Oh, for the very ruth thine eyes have told,
Answer the rune this love of thee hath taught me.

V

After an age of longing had we missed
Our meeting and the dream, what were the good
Of weaving cloth of words? Were jewelled tales
An opiate meet to quell the malady
Of life unlived? In untried monotone
Were not the earth as vain, and dry, and old,
For thee, O Perfect Light, had I not sought thee?

VI

Calais, in song where word and tone keep tryst
Behold my heart, and hear mine hardihood!
Calais, the wind is come and heaven pales
And trembles for the love of day to be.
Calais, the words break and the dawn is shown.
Ah, but the stars set when thou wast first bold,
Turn! lest they say a lesser light distraught thee.

VII

O ivory thou, the golden scythe hath mown
Night's stubble and my joy. Thou royal souled,
Favour the quest! Lo, Truth and I have sought thee!

OCTAVE

Fine songs, fair songs, these golden usuries
Her beauty earns as but just increment,
And they do speak with a most ill intent
Who say they give when they pay debtor's fees.

I call him bankrupt in the courts of song
Who hath her gold to eye and pays her not,
Defaulter do I call the knave who hath got
Her silver in his heart, and doth her wrong.

SONNET

If on the tally-board of wasted days
They daily write me for proud idleness,
Let high Hell summons me, and I confess,
No overt act the preferred charge allays.

To-day I thought—what boots it what I thought?
Poppies and gold! Why should I blurt it out?
Or hawk the magic of her name about
Deaf doors and dungeons where no truth is bought?

Who calls me idle? I have thought of her.
Who calls me idle? By God's truth I've seen
The arrowy sunlight in her golden snares.

Let him among you all stand summonser
Who hath done better things! Let whoso hath been
With worthier works concerned, display his wares!

BALLATETTA

The light became her grace and dwelt among
Blind eyes and shadows that are formed as men;
Lo, how the light doth melt us into song:

The broken sunlight for a healm she beareth
Who hath my heart in jurisdiction.
In wild-wood never fawn nor fallow fareth
So silent light; no gossamer is spun
So delicate as she is, when the sun
Drives the clear emeralds from the bended grasses
Lest they should parch too swiftly, where she passes.

MADRIGALE

Clear is my love but shadowed
By the spun gold above her,
Ah, what a petal those bent sheaths discover!

The olive wood hath hidden her completely,
She was gowned that discreetly
The leaves and shadows concealed her completely.

Fair is my love but followed
In all her goings surely
By gracious thoughts, she goeth so demurely.

ERA MEA

Era mea
In qua terra
Dulce myrti floribus,
Rosa amoris
Via erroris
Ad te coram
Veniam?

ANGLICÈ REDDITA
Mistress mine, in what far land,
Where the myrtle bloweth sweet
Shall I weary with my way-fare,
Win to thee that art as day fair,
Lay my roses at thy feet?

PARACELSUS IN EXCELSIS

"Being no longer human why should I
Pretend humanity or don the frail attire?
Men have I known, and men, but never one
Was grown so free an essence, or become
So simply element as what I am.
The mist goes from the mirror and I see!
Behold! the world of forms is swept beneath—
Turmoil grown visible beneath our peace,
And we, that are grown formless, rise above—
Fluids intangible that have been men,
We seem as statues round whose high-risen base
Some overflowing river is run mad,
In us alone the element of calm!"

148

PRAYER FOR HIS LADY'S LIFE

From Propertius, *Elegiae,* Lib. III, 26

Here let thy clemency, Persephone, hold firm,
Do thou, Pluto, bring here no greater harshness.
So many thousand beauties are gone down to Avernus
Ye might let one remain above with us.

With you is Iope, with you the white-gleaming Tyro,
With you is Europa and the shameless Pasiphae,
And all the fair from Troy and all from Achaia,
From the sundered realms, of Thebes and of aged Priamus;
And all the maidens of Rome, as many as they were,
They died and the greed of your flame consumes them.

  Here let thy clemency, Persephone, hold firm,
  Do thou, Pluto, bring here no greater harshness.
  So many thousand fair are gone down to Avernus,
  Ye might let one remain above with us.

SPEECH FOR PSYCHE
IN THE GOLDEN BOOK OF APULEIUS

All night, and as the wind lieth among
The cypress trees, he lay,
Nor held me save as air that brusheth by one
Close, and as the petals of flowers in falling
Waver and seem not drawn to earth, so he
Seemed over me to hover light as leaves
And closer me than air,
And music flowing through me seemed to open
Mine eyes upon new colours.
O winds, what wind can match the weight of him!

"BLANDULA, TENULLA, VAGULA"

What hast thou, O my soul, with paradise?
Will we not rather, when our freedom's won,
Get us to some clear place wherein the sun
Lets drift in on us through the olive leaves
A liquid glory? If at Sirmio
My soul, I meet thee, when this life's outrun,
Will we not find some headland consecrated
By aery apostles of terrene delight,
Will not our cult be founded on the waves,
Clear sapphire, cobalt, cyanine,
On triune azures, the impalpable
Mirrors unstill of the eternal change?

Soul, if She meet us there, will any rumour
Of havens more high and courts desirable
Lure us beyond the cloudy peak of Riva?

ERAT HORA

"Thank you, whatever comes." And then she turned
And, as the ray of sun on hanging flowers
Fades when the wind hath lifted them aside,
Went swiftly from me. Nay, whatever comes
One hour was sunlit and the most high gods
May not make boast of any better thing
Than to have watched that hour as it passed.

EPIGRAMS

O ivory, delicate hands!
O face that hovers
Between "To-come" and "Was,"
Ivory thou wast,
A rose thou wilt be.

(THE SEA OF GLASS)

I looked and saw a sea
               roofed over with rainbows,
In the midst of each
               two lovers met and departed;
Then the sky was full of faces
               with gold glories behind them.

LA NUVOLETTA

Dante to an unknown lady, beseeching her not to interrupt
his cult of the dead Beatrice. From "Il Canzoniere," Ballata II.

Ah little cloud that in Love's shadow lief
Upon mine eyes so suddenly alightest,
Take some faint pity on the heart thou smitest
That hopes in thee, desires, dies, in brief.

Ah little cloud of more than human fashion
Thou settest a flame within my mind's mid space
With thy deathly speech that grieveth;

Then as a fiery spirit in thy ways
Createst hope, in part a rightful passion,

Yet where thy sweet smile giveth
His grace, look not! For in Her my faith liveth.

Think on my high desire whose flame's so great
That nigh a thousand who were come too late,
Have felt the torment of another's grief.

ROSA SEMPITERNA

A rose I set within my "Paradise"
Lo how his red is turned to yellowness,
Not withered but grown old in subtler wise
Between the empaged rime's high holiness
Where Dante sings of that rose's device
Which yellow is, with souls in blissfulness.
Rose whom I set within my paradise,
Donor of roses and of parching sighs,
Of golden lights and dark unhappiness,
Of hidden chains and silvery joyousness,
Hear how thy rose within my Dante lies,
O rose I set within my paradise.

THE GOLDEN SESTINA

From the Italian of Pico della Mirandola

In the bright season when He, most high Jove,
From welkin reaching down his glorying hand,
Decks the Great Mother and her changing face,
Clothing her not with scarlet skeins and gold
But with th' empurpling flowers and gay grass,
When the young year renewed, renews the sun,

When, then, I see a lady like the sun,
One fashioned by th' high hand of utmost Jove,
So fair beneath the myrtles on gay grass
Who holdeth Love and Truth, one by each hand,
It seems, if I look straight, two bands of gold
Do make more fair her delicate fair face.

Though eyes are dazzled, looking on her face
As all sight faileth that looks toward the sun,
New metamorphoses, to rained gold,
Or bulls or whitest swans, might fall on Jove
Through her, or Phoebus, his bag-pipes in hand,
Might, mid the droves, come barefoot o'er our grass.

Alas, that there was hidden in the grass
A cruel shaft, the which, to wound my face,
My Lady took in her own proper hand.
If I could not defend me 'gainst that sun
I take no shame, for even utmost Jove
Is in high heaven pierced with darts of gold.

Behold the green shall find itself turned gold
And spring shall be without her flowers and grass,
And hell's deep be the dwelling place of Jove
Ere I shall have uncarved her holy face
From my heart's midst, where 'tis both Sun and sun;
And yet she beareth me such hostile hand!

O sweet and holy and O most light hand,
O intermingled ivory and gold,
O mortal goddess and terrestrial sun
Who comest not to foster meadow grass,
But to show heaven by a likened face
Wert sent amongst us by th' exalted Jove,

I still pray Jove that he permit no grass
To cover o'er thy hands, thy face, thy gold
For heaven's sufficèd with a single sun.

ROME

From the French of Joachim du Bellay
"Troica Roma resurges."
PROPERTIUS

O thou new comer who seek'st Rome in Rome
And find'st in Rome no thing thou canst call Roman;
Arches worn old and palaces made common,
Rome's name alone within these walls keeps home.

Behold how pride and ruin can befall
One who hath set the whole world 'neath her laws,
All-conquering, now conquerèd, because
She is Time's prey and Time consumeth all.

Rome that art Rome's one sole last monument,
Rome that alone hast conquered Rome the town,
Tiber alone, transient and seaward bent,
Remains of Rome. O world, thou unconstant mime!
That which stands firm in thee Time batters down,
And that which fleeteth doth outrun swift time.

HER MONUMENT, THE IMAGE CUT THEREON

From the Italian of Leopardi (Written 1831–3 circa)

Such wast thou,
Who art now
But buried dust and rusted skeleton.
Above the bones and mire,
Motionless, placed in vain,
Mute mirror of the flight of speeding years,
Sole guard of grief
Sole guard of memory
Standeth this image of the beauty sped.

O glance, when thou wast still as thou art now,
How hast thou set the fire
A-tremble in men's veins; O lip curved high
To mind me of some urn of full delight,
O throat girt round of old with swift desire,
O palms of Love, that in your wonted ways
Not once but many a day
Felt hands turn ice a-sudden, touching ye,
That ye were once! of all the grace ye had
That which remaineth now
Shameful, most sad
Finds 'neath this rock fit mould, fit resting place!

And still when fate recalleth,
Even that semblance that appears amongst us
Is like to heaven's most 'live imagining.
All, all our life's eternal mystery!
To-day, on high
Mounts, from our mighty thoughts and from the fount
Of sense untellable, Beauty
That seems to be some quivering splendour cast
By the immortal nature on this quicksand,
And by surhuman fates
Given to mortal state
To be a sign and an hope made secure
Of blissful kingdoms and the aureate spheres;
And on the morrow, by some lightsome twist,
Shameful in sight, abject, abominable
All this angelic aspect can return
And be but what it was
With all the admirable concepts that moved from it
Swept from the mind with it in its departure.

Infinite things desired, lofty visions
'Got on desirous thought by natural virtue,
And the wise concord, whence through delicious seas
The arcane spirit of the whole Mankind
Turns hardy pilot . . . and if one wrong note
Strike the tympanum,

Instantly
That paradise is hurled to nothingness.

O mortal nature,
If thou art
Frail and so vile in all,
How canst thou reach so high with thy poor sense;
Yet if thou art
Noble in any part
How is the noblest of thy speech and thought
So lightly wrought
Or to such base occasion lit and quenched?

VICTORIAN ECLOGUES

I
EXCUSES

Ah would you turn me back now from the flowers,
You who are different as the air from sea is,
Ah for the pollen from our wreath of hours,
You who are magical, not mine as she is,
Say will you call us from our time of flowers?

You whom I loved and love, not understanding,
Yea we were ever torn with constant striving,
Seeing our gods are different, and commanding
One good from them, and in my heart reviving
Old discords and bent thought, not understanding.

We who have wept, we who have lain together
Upon the green and sere and white of every season,
We who have loved the sun but for the weather
Of our own hearts have found no constant reason,
What is your part, now *we* have come together?

What is your pain, Dear, what is your heart now
A little sad, a little . . . . . Nay, I know not
Seeing I never had and have no part now
In your own secret councils wherein blow not
My roses. My vineyard being another heart now?

You who were ever dear and dearer being strange,
How shall I "go" who never came anear you?
How could I stay, who never came in range
Of anything that halved; could never hear you
Rightly in your silence; nay, your very speech was strange.

You, who have loved not what I was or will be,
You who but loved me for a thing I could be,
You who love not a song whate'er its skill be
But only love the cause or what cause should be,
How could I give you what I am or will be?

Nay, though your eyes are sad, you will not hinder,
You, who would have had me only near not nearer,
Nay though my heart had burned to a bright cinder
Love would have said to me: "Still fear her,
Pain is thy lot and naught she hath can hinder."

So I, for this sad gladness that is mine now,
Who never spoke aright in speaking to you,
Uncomprehending anything that's thine now,
E'en in my spoken words more wrong may do you
In looking back from this new grace that's mine now.

Sic semper finis deest.

II
SATIEMUS

What if I know thy speeches word by word?
And if thou knew'st I knew them wouldst thou speak?
What if I know thy speeches word by word,
And all the time thou sayest them o'er I said,
"Lo, one there was who bent her fair bright head,

Sighing as thou dost through the golden speech."
Or, as our laughters mingle each with each,
As crushed lips take their respite fitfully,
What if my thoughts were turned in their mid reach
Whispering among them, "The fair dead
Must know such moments, thinking on the grass;
Oh how white dogwoods murmured overhead
In the bright glad days!"
How if the low dear sound within thy throat
Hath as faint lute-strings in its dim accord
Dim tales that blind me, running one by one
With times told over as we tell by rote;
What if I know thy laughter word by word
Nor find aught novel in thy merriment?

III

ABELARD
"Pere Esbaillart a Sanct Denis." Villon
"Because my soul cried out, and only the long ways
Grown weary, gave me answer and
Because she answered when the very ways were dumb
With all their hoarse, dry speech grown faint and chill.
Because her answer was a call to me,
Though I have sinned, my God, and though thy angels
Bear no more now my thought to whom I love;
Now though I crouch afraid in all thy dark
Will I once cry to thee:
                    Once more! Once more my strength!
Yea though I sin to call him forth once more,
Thy messengers for mine,
Their wings my power!
And let once more my wings fold down above her,
Let their cool length be spread
Over her feet and head
And let thy calm come down
To dwell within her, and thy gown of peace
Clothe all her body in its samite.
O Father of all the blind and all the strong,
Though I have left thy courts, though all the throng
Of thy gold-shimmering choir know me not,

Though I have dared the body and have donned
Its frail strong-seeming, and although
Its lightening joy is made my swifter song,
Though I have known thy stars, yea all,
      and chosen one.
Yea though I make no barter, and repent no jot,
Yet for the sunlight of that former time
Grant me the boon, O God,
Once more, once more, or I or some white thought
Shall rise beside her and, enveloping
All her strange glory in its wings of light,
Bring down thy peace upon her way-worn soul.
Oh sheathe that sword of her in some strong case,
The doe-skin scabbard of thy clear Rafael!
Yea let thy angels walk, as I have seen
Them passing, or have seen their wings
Spread their pavilions o'er our twin delight.
Yea I have seen them when the purple light
Hid all her garden from my drowsy eyes.

A PROLOGUE

The Lords of the Air:
    What light hath passed us in the silent ways?

The Spirits of Fire:
    We are sustainèd, strengthened suddenly.

The Spirits of Water:
    Lo, how the utmost deeps are clarified!

The Spirits Terrene:
    What might is this more potent than the spring?
    Lo, how the night

Which wrapped us round with its most heavy cloths
Opens and breathes with some strange-fashioned
    brightness!

*Christ, the eternal Spirit in Heaven speaketh thus, over
    the child of Mary:*
    O star, move forth and write upon the skies,
    "This child is born in ways miraculous."

                . . . . .

    O windy spirits, that are born in Heaven,
    Go down and bid the powers of Earth and Air
    Protect his ways until the Time shall come.

                . . . . .

    O Mother, if the dark of things to be
    Wrap round thy heart with cloudy apprehensions,
    Eat of thy present corn, the aftermath
    Hath its appointed end in whirling light.
    Eat of thy present corn, thou so hast share
    In mightier portents than Augustus hath.

                . . .

    In every moment all to be is born,
    Thou art the moment and need'st fear no scorn.

Echo of the Angels singing "Exultasti:"
    Silence is born of many peaceful things,
    Thus is the starlight woven into strings
    Whereon the Powers of peace make sweet accord.
    Rejoice, O Earth, thy Lord
    Hath chosen Him his holy resting-place.

    Lo, how the wingèd sign
    Flutters above that hallowed chrysalis.

The invisible Spirit of the Star answers them:
    Bend in your singing, gracious potencies,
    Bend low above your ivory bows and gold!
    That which ye know but dimly hath been wrought
    High in the luminous courts and azure ways:

Bend in your praise;
For though your subtle thought
Sees but in part the source of mysteries,
Yet are ye bidden in your songs, sing this:

> "Gloria! gloria in excelsis
> Pax in terra nunc natast."

Angels continuing in song:
Shepherds and kings, with lambs and frankincense
Go and atone for mankind's ignorance:
Make ye soft savour from your ruddy myrrh.
Lo, how God's son is turned God's almoner.
Give ye this little
Ere he give ye all.

ON EARTH

One of the Magi:
How the deep-voicèd night turns councillor!
And how, for end, our starry meditations
Admit us to his board!

A Shepherd:
Sir, we be humble and perceive ye are
Men of great power and authority,
And yet we too have heard.

DIANA IN EPHESUS

(Lucina dolentibus:)
"Behold the deed! Behold the act supreme!
With mine own hands have I prepared my doom,
Truth shall grow great eclipsing other truth,
And men forget me in the aging years.
Explicit.

MAESTRO DI TOCAR

(W. R.)

You, who are touched not by our mortal ways
Nor girded with the stricture of our bands,
Have but to loose the magic from your hands
And all men's hearts that glimmer for a day,
And all our loves that are so swift to flame
Rise in that space of sound and melt away.

ARIA

My love is a deep flame
                that hides beneath the waters.

—My love is gay and kind,
My love is hard to find
          as the flame beneath the waters.

The fingers of the wind
                      meet hers
With a frail
             swift greeting.
My love is gay
              and kind
                    and hard
                            of meeting,
As the flame beneath the waters
             hard of meeting.

L'ART

When brightest colours seem but dull in hue
And noblest arts are shown mechanical,
When study serves but to heap clue on clue
That no great line hath been or ever shall,
But hath a savour like some second stew
Of many pot-lots with a smack of all.
'Twas one man's field, another's hops the brew,
'Twas vagrant accident not fate's fore-call.

Horace, that thing of thine is overhauled,
And "Wood notes wild" weaves a concocted sonnet.
Here aery Shelley on the text hath called,
And here, Great Scott, the Murex, Keats comes on it.
And all the lot howl, "Sweet Simplicity!"
'Tis Art to hide our theft exquisitely.

SONG IN THE MANNER OF HOUSMAN

O woe, woe,
People are born and die,
We also shall be dead pretty soon
Therefore let us act as if we were
                    dead already.

The bird sits on the hawthorn tree
But he dies also, presently.
Some lads get hung, and some get shot.
Woeful is this human lot.
                    Woe! woe, etcetera . . . .

London is a woeful place,
Shropshire is much pleasanter.

Then let us smile a little space
Upon fond nature's morbid grace.
                    Oh, Woe, woe, woe, etcetera . . . .

TRANSLATIONS FROM HEINE

Von "Die Heimkehr"

I
Is your hate, then, of such measure?
Do you, truly, so detest me?
Through all the world will I complain
Of *how* you have addressed me.

O ye lips that are ungrateful,
Hath it never once distressed you,
That you can say such *awful* things
Of *any* one who ever kissed you?

II
So thou hast forgotten fully
That I so long held thy heart wholly,
Thy little heart, so sweet and false and small
That there's no thing more sweet or false at all.

Love and lay thou hast forgotten fully,
And my heart worked at them unduly.
I know not if the love or if the lay were better stuff,
But I know now, they both were good enough.

III
Tell me where thy lovely love is,
Whom thou once did sing so sweetly,
When the fairy flames enshrouded
Thee, and held thy heart completely.

All the flames are dead and sped now
And my heart is cold and sere;
Behold this book, the urn of ashes,
'Tis my true love's sepulchre.

IV

I dreamt that I was God Himself
Whom heavenly joy immerses,
And all the angels sat about
And praised my verses.

V

The mutilated choir boys
When I begin to sing
Complain about the awful noise
And call my voice too thick a thing.

When light their voices lift them up,
Bright notes against the ear,
Through trills and runs like crystal,
Ring delicate and clear.

They sing of Love that's grown desirous,
Of Love, and joy that is Love's inmost part,
And all the ladies swim through tears
Toward such a work of art.

VI

This delightful young man
Should not lack for honourers,
He propitiates me with oysters,
With Rhine wine and liqueurs.

How his coat and pants adorn him!
Yet his ties are more adorning,
In these he daily comes to ask me:
Are you feeling well this morning?

He speaks of my extended fame,
My wit, charm, definitions,

And is diligent to serve me,
Is detailed in his provisions.

In evening company he sets his face
In most spiritu*el* positions,
And declaims before the ladies
My *god-like* compositions.

O what comfort is it for me
To find him such, when the days bring
No comfort, at my time of life when
All good things go vanishing.

Translator to Translated

O Harry Heine, curses be,
I live too late to sup with thee!
Who can demolish at such polished ease
Philistia's pomp and Art's pomposities!

VII
SONG FROM "DIE HARZREISE"

I am the Princess Ilza
In Ilsenstein I fare,
Come with me to that castle
And we'll be happy there.

Thy head will I cover over
With my waves' clarity
Till thou forget thy sorrow,
O wounded sorrowfully.

Thou wilt in my white arms there,
Nay, on my breast thou must
Forget and rest and dream there
For thine old legend-lust.

My lips and my heart are thine there
As they were his and mine.

His? Why the good King Harry's,
And he is dead lang syne.

Dead men stay alway dead men,
Life is the live man's part,
And I am fair and golden
With joy breathless at heart.

If my heart stay below there,
My crystal halls ring clear
To the dance of lords and ladies
In all their splendid gear.

The silken trains go rustling,
The spur-clinks sound between,
The dark dwarfs blow and bow there
Small horn and violin.

Yet shall my white arms hold thee,
That bound King Harry about.
Ah, I covered his ears with them
When the trumpet rang out.

UND DRANG

> Nay, dwells he in cloudy rumour alone?
> Binyon

I

I am worn faint,
The winds of good and evil
Blind me with dust
And burn me with the cold,
There is no comfort being over-man;
Yet are we come more near

The great oblivions and the labouring night,
Inchoate truth and the sepulchral forces.

II

Confusion, clamour, 'mid the many voices
Is there a meaning, a significance?

That life apart from all life gives and takes,
This life, apart from all life's bitter and life's sweet,
Is good.
                    Ye see me and ye say: exceeding sweet
Life's gifts, his youth, his art,
And his too soon acclaim.

I also knew exceeding bitterness,
Saw good things altered and old friends fare forth,
And what I loved in me hath died too soon,
Yea I have seen the "gray above the green";
Gay have I lived in life;
                              Though life hath lain
Strange hands upon me and hath torn my sides,
Yet I believe.
                    .   .   .   .   .   .

Life is most cruel where she is most wise.

III

The will to live goes from me.
                              I have lain
Dull and out-worn
                    with some strange, subtle sickness.
Who shall say
That love is not the very root of this,
O thou afar?

Yet she was near me,
                    that eternal deep.
O it is passing strange that love
Can blow two ways across one soul.

                    .   .   .   .   .   .

And I was Aengus for a thousand years,

168

And she, the ever-living, moved with me
And strove amid the waves, and

                    would not go.

ELEGIA

"Far buon tempo e trionfare"
"I have put my days and dreams out of mind"
For all their hurry and their weary fret
Availed me little. But another kind
Of leaf that's fast in some more sombre wind,
Is man on life, and all our tenuous courses
Wind and unwind as vainly.

                . . . . .

I have lived long, and died,
Yea I have been dead, right often,
And have seen one thing:
The sun, while he is high, doth light our wrong
And none can break the darkness with a song.

To-day's the cup. To-morrow is not ours:
Nay, by our strongest bands we bind her not,
Nor all our fears and our anxieties
Turn her one leaf or hold her scimitar.

The deed blots out the thought
And many thoughts, the vision;
And right's a compass with as many poles
As there are points in her circumference,
'Tis vain to seek to steer all courses even,
And all things save sheer right are vain enough.
The blade were vain to grow save toward the sun,
And vain th' attempt to hold her green forever.

All things in season and no thing o'er long!
Love and desire and gain and good forgetting,
Thou canst not stay the wheel, hold none too long!

                    V

How our modernity,
Nerve-wracked and broken, turns

169

Against time's way and all the way of things,
Crying with weak and egoistic cries!

. . . . .

All things are given over,
Only the restless will
Surges amid the stars
Seeking new moods of life,
New permutations.

. . . . .

See, and the very sense of what we know
Dodges and hides as in a sombre curtain
Bright threads leap forth, and hide, and leave no pattern.

VI

I thought I had put Love by for a time
And I was glad, for to me his fair face
Is like Pain's face.
                    A little light,
The lowered curtain and the theatre!
And o'er the frail talk of the inter-act
Something that broke the jest! A little light,
The gold, and half the profile!
                                    The whole face
Was nothing like you, yet that image cut
Sheer through the moment.

VIb

I have gone seeking for you in the twilight,
Here in the flurry of Fifth Avenue,
Here where they pass between their teas and teas.
Is it such madness? though you could not be
Ever in all that crowd, no gown
Of all their subtle sorts could be your gown.

Yet I am fed with faces, is there one
That even in the half-light mindeth me.

VII
THE HOUSE OF SPLENDOUR

'Tis Evanoe's,
A house not made with hands,

But out somewhere beyond the worldly ways
Her gold is spread, above, around, inwoven,
Strange ways and walls are fashioned out of it.

And I have seen my Lady in the sun,
Her hair was spread about, a sheaf of wings,
And red the sunlight was, behind it all.

And I have seen her there within her house,
With six great sapphires hung along the wall,
Low, panel-shaped, a-level with her knees,
And all her robe was woven of pale gold.

There are there many rooms and all of gold,
Of woven walls deep patterned, of email,
Of beaten work; and through the claret stone,
Set to some weaving, comes the aureate light.

Here am I come perforce my love of her,
Behold mine adoration
Maketh me clear, and there are powers in this
Which, played on by the virtues of her soul,
Break down the four-square walls of standing time.

VIII
THE FLAME

'Tis not a game that plays at mates and mating,
Provençe knew;
'Tis not a game of barter, lands and houses,
Provençe knew.
We who are wise beyond your dream of wisdom,
Drink our immortal moments; we "pass through."
We have gone forth beyond your bonds and borders,
Provençe knew;
And all the tales they ever writ of Oisin
Say but this:
That man doth pass the net of days and hours.
Where time is shrivelled down to time's seed corn
We of the Ever-living, in that light
Meet through our veils and whisper, and of love.

O smoke and shadow of a darkling world,
Barters of passion, and that tenderness
That's but a sort of cunning! O my Love,
These, and the rest, and all the rest we knew.

'Tis not a game that plays at mates and mating,
'Tis not a game of barter, lands and houses,
'Tis not "of days and nights" and troubling years,
Of cheeks grown sunken and glad hair gone gray;
There *is* the subtler music, the clear light
Where time burns back about th' eternal embers.
We are not shut from all the thousand heavens:
Lo, there are many gods whom we have seen,
Folk of unearthly fashion, places splendid,
Bulwarks of beryl and of chrysoprase.

Sapphire Benacus, in thy mists and thee
Nature herself's turned metaphysical,
Who can look on that blue and not believe?

Thou hooded opal, thou eternal pearl,
O thou dark secret with a shimmering floor,
Through all thy various mood I know thee mine;

If I have merged my soul, or utterly
Am solved and bound in, through aught here on earth,
There canst thou find me, O thou anxious thou,
Who call'st about my gates for some lost me;
I say my soul flowed back, became translucent.
Search not my lips, O Love, let go my hands,
This thing that moves as man is no more mortal.
If thou hast seen my shade sans character,
If thou hast seen that mirror of all moments,
That glass to all things that o'ershadow it,
Call not that mirror me, for I have slipped
Your grasp, I have eluded.

IX
(HORAE BEATAE INSCRIPTIO)
How will this beauty, when I am far hence,
Sweep back upon me and engulf my mind!

How will these hours, when we twain are gray,
Turned in their sapphire tide, come flooding o'er us!

X
(THE ALTAR)
Let us build here an exquisite friendship,
The flame, the autumn, and the green rose of love
Fought out their strife here, 'tis a place of wonder;
Where these have been, meet 'tis, the ground is holy.

XI
(AU SALON)
> Her grave, sweet haughtiness
> Pleaseth me, and in like wise
> Her quiet ironies.
> Others are beautiful, none more, some less.

I suppose, when poetry comes down to facts,
When our souls are returned to the gods
                    and the spheres they belong in,
Here in the every-day where our acts
Rise up and judge us;

I suppose there are a few dozen verities
That no shift of mood can shake from us:

One place where we'd rather have tea
(Thus far hath modernity brought us)
"Tea" (Damn you!)
                    Have tea, damn the Caesars,
Talk of the latest success, give wing to some scandal,
Garble a name we detest, and for prejudice?
Set loose the whole consummate pack
                    to bay like Sir Roger de Coverley's.

This our reward for our works,
                    sic crescit gloria mundi:
Some circle of not more than three
                    that we prefer to play up to,

Some few whom we'd rather please
          than hear the whole aegrum vulgus

Splitting its beery jowl
            a-meaowling our praises.

Some certain peculiar things,
            cari laresque, penates,
Some certain accustomed forms,
            the absolute unimportant.

XII

(AU JARDIN)

O you away high there,
            you that lean
From amber lattices upon the cobalt night,
I am below amid the pine trees,
Amid the little pine trees, hear me!

"The jester walked in the garden."
                        Did he so?
Well, there's no use your loving me
That way, Lady;
For I've nothing but songs to give you.

I am set wide upon the world's ways
To say that life is, some way, a gay thing,
But you never string two days upon one wire
But there'll come sorrow of it.
                        And I loved a love once,
Over beyond the moon there,
                        I loved a love once,
And, may be, more times,

But she danced like a pink moth in the shrubbery.

Oh, I know you women from the "other folk,"
And it'll all come right,
O' Sundays.

"The jester walked in the garden."
                        Did he so?

RIPOSTES

1912

RIPOSTES

OF

EZRA POUND

WHERETO ARE APPENDED
THE COMPLETE POETICAL
WORKS OF

T. E. HULME

WITH PREFATORY NOTE

MCMXII
STEPHEN SWIFT AND CO., LTD.
16 KING STREET, COVENT GARDEN
LONDON

Title page of Ripostes, *London, 1912*

Gird on thy star, We'll have this out with fate.

SILET

When I behold how black, immortal ink
Drips from my deathless pen—ah, well-away!
Why should we stop at all for what I think?
There is enough in what I chance to say.

It is enough that we once came together;
What is the use of setting it to rime?
When it is autumn do we get spring weather,
Or gather may of harsh northwindish time?

It is enough that we once came together;
What if the wind have turned against the rain?
It is enough that we once came together;
Time has seen this, and will not turn again;

And who are we, who know that last intent,
To plague to-morrow with a testament!

IN EXITUM CUIUSDAM

On a certain one's departure

"Time's bitter flood"! Oh, that's all very well,
But where's the old friend hasn't fallen off,
Or slacked his hand-grip when you first gripped fame?

I know your circle and can fairly tell
What you have kept and what you've left behind:
I know my circle and know very well
How many faces I'd have out of mind.

APPARUIT

Golden rose the house, in the portal I saw
thee, a marvel, carven in subtle stuff, a
portent. Life died down in the lamp and flickered,
        caught at the wonder.

Crimson, frosty with dew, the roses bend where
thou afar moving in the glamorous sun
drinkst in life of earth, of the air, the tissue
        golden about thee.

Green the ways, the breath of the fields is thine there,
open lies the land, yet the steely going
darkly hast thou dared and the dreaded æther
        parted before thee.

Swift at courage thou in the shell of gold, cast-
ing a-loose the cloak of the body, camest
straight, then shone thine oriel and the stunned light
        faded about thee.

Half the graven shoulder, the throat aflash with
strands of light inwoven about it, loveli-
est of all things, frail alabaster, ah me!
      swift in departing,

Clothed in goldish weft, delicately perfect,
gone as wind! The cloth of the magical hands!
Thou a slight thing, thou in access of cunning
      dar'dst to assume this?

THE TOMB AT AKR ÇAAR

"I am thy soul, Nikoptis. I have watched
These five millennia, and thy dead eyes
Moved not, nor ever answer my desire,
And thy light limbs, wherethrough I leapt aflame,
Burn not with me nor any saffron thing.

See, the light grass sprang up to pillow thee,
And kissed thee with a myriad grassy tongues;
But not thou me.

I have read out the gold upon the wall,
And wearied out my thought upon the signs.
And there is no new thing in all this place.

I have been kind. See, I have left the jars sealed,
Lest thou shouldst wake and whimper for thy wine.
And all thy robes I have kept smooth on thee.

O thou unmindful! How should I forget!
—Even the river many days ago,
The river, thou wast over young.
And three souls came upon Thee—

And I came.
And I flowed in upon thee, beat them off;
I have been intimate with thee, known thy ways.
Have I not touched thy palms and finger-tips,
Flowed in, and through thee and about thy heels?
How 'came I in'? Was I not thee and Thee?

And no sun comes to rest me in this place,
And I am torn against the jagged dark,
And no light beats upon me, and you say
No word, day after day.

Oh! I could get me out, despite the marks
And all their crafty work upon the door,
Out through the glass-green fields . . . .

.   .   .   .

Yet it is quiet here:
I do not go."

PORTRAIT D'UNE FEMME

Your mind and you are our Sargasso Sea,
London has swept about you this score years
And bright ships left you this or that in fee:
Ideas, old gossip, oddments of all things,
Strange spars of knowledge and dimmed wares of price.
Great minds have sought you—lacking someone else.
You have been second always. Tragical?
No. You preferred it to the usual thing:
One dull man, dulling and uxorious,
One average mind—with one thought less, each year.
Oh, you are patient, I have seen you sit
Hours, where something might have floated up.
And now you pay one. Yes, you richly pay.
You are a person of some interest, one comes to you

And takes strange gain away:
Trophies fished up; some curious suggestion;
Fact that leads nowhere; and a tale for two,
Pregnant with mandrakes, or with something else
That might prove useful and yet never proves,
That never fits a corner or shows use,
Or finds its hour upon the loom of days:
The tarnished, gaudy, wonderful old work;
Idols and ambergris and rare inlays,
These are your riches, your great store; and yet
For all this sea-hoard of deciduous things,
Strange woods half sodden, and new brighter stuff:
In the slow float of differing light and deep,
No! there is nothing! In the whole and all,
Nothing that's quite your own.
                    Yet this is you.

N.Y.

My City, my beloved, my white! Ah, slender,
Listen! Listen to me, and I will breathe into thee a soul.
Delicately upon the reed, attend me!

Now do I know that I am mad,
For here are a million people surly with traffic;
This is no maid.
Neither could I play upon any reed if I had one.

My City, my beloved,
Thou art a maid with no breasts,
Thou art slender as a silver reed.
Listen to me, attend me!
And I will breathe into thee a soul,
And thou shalt live for ever.

A GIRL

The tree has entered my hands,
The sap has ascended my arms,
The tree has grown in my breast—
Downward,
The branches grow out of me, like arms.

Tree you are,
Moss you are,
You are violets with wind above them.
A child—*so* high—you are,
And all this is folly to the world.

"PHASELLUS ILLE"

This *papier-mâché*, which you see, my friends,
Saith 'twas the worthiest of editors.
Its mind was made up in "the seventies,"
Nor hath it ever since changed that concoction.
It works to represent that school of thought
Which brought the hair-cloth chair to such perfection,
Nor will the horrid threats of Bernard Shaw
Shake up the stagnant pool of its convictions;
Nay, should the deathless voice of all the world
Speak once again for its sole stimulation,
'Twould not move it one jot from left to right.

Come Beauty barefoot from the Cyclades,
She'd find a model for St. Anthony
In this thing's sure *decorum* and behaviour.

AN OBJECT

This thing, that hath a code and not a core,
Hath set acquaintance where might be affections,
And nothing now
Disturbeth his reflections.

QUIES

This is another of our ancient loves.
Pass and be silent, Rullus, for the day
Hath lacked a something since this lady passed;
Hath lacked a something. 'Twas but marginal.

THE SEAFARER

(From the early Anglo-Saxon text)

May I for my own self song's truth reckon,
Journey's jargon, how I in harsh days
Hardship endured oft.
Bitter breast-cares have I abided,
Known on my keel many a care's hold,
And dire sea-surge, and there I oft spent
Narrow nightwatch nigh the ship's head
While she tossed close to cliffs. Coldly afflicted,
My feet were by frost benumbed.
Chill its chains are; chafing sighs
Hew my heart round and hunger begot
Mere-weary mood. Lest man know not
That he on dry land loveliest liveth,
List how I, care-wretched, on ice-cold sea,
Weathered the winter, wretched outcast
Deprived of my kinsmen;
Hung with hard ice-flakes, where hail-scur flew,
There I heard naught save the harsh sea
And ice-cold wave, at whiles the swan cries,
Did for my games the gannet's clamour,
Sea-fowls' loudness was for me laughter,
The mews' singing all my mead-drink.
Storms, on the stone-cliffs beaten, fell on the stern
In icy feathers; full oft the eagle screamed
With spray on his pinion.
                          Not any protector
May make merry man faring needy.
This he little believes, who aye in winsome life
Abides 'mid burghers some heavy business,
Wealthy and wine-flushed, how I weary oft
Must bide above brine.
Neareth nightshade, snoweth from north,
Frost froze the land, hail fell on earth then
Corn of the coldest. Nathless there knocketh now
The heart's thought that I on high streams

The salt-wavy tumult traverse alone.
Moaneth alway my mind's lust
That I fare forth, that I afar hence
Seek out a foreign fastness.
For this there's no mood-lofty man over earth's midst,
Not though he be given his good, but will have in his youth greed;
Nor his deed to the daring, nor his king to the faithful
But shall have his sorrow for sea-fare
Whatever his lord will.
He hath not heart for harping, nor in ring-having
Nor winsomeness to wife, nor world's delight
Nor any whit else save the wave's slash,
Yet longing comes upon him to fare forth on the water.
Bosque taketh blossom, cometh beauty of berries,
Fields to fairness, land fares brisker,
All this admonisheth man eager of mood,
The heart turns to travel so that he then thinks
On flood-ways to be far departing.
Cuckoo calleth with gloomy crying,
He singeth summerward, bodeth sorrow,
The bitter heart's blood. Burgher knows not—
He the prosperous man—what some perform
Where wandering them widest draweth.
So that but now my heart burst from my breast-lock,
My mood 'mid the mere-flood,
Over the whale's acre, would wander wide.
On earth's shelter cometh often to me,
Eager and ready, the crying lone-flyer,
Whets for the whale-path the heart irresistibly,
O'er tracks of ocean; seeing that anyhow
My lord deems to me this dead life
On loan and on land, I believe not
That any earth-weal eternal standeth
Save there be somewhat calamitous
That, ere a man's tide go, turn it to twain.
Disease or oldness or sword-hate
Beats out the breath from doom-gripped body.
And for this, every earl whatever, for those speaking after—
Laud of the living, boasteth some last word,

That he will work ere he pass onward,
Frame on the fair earth 'gainst foes his malice,
Daring ado, . . .
So that all men shall honour him after
And his laud beyond them remain 'mid the English,
Aye, for ever, a lasting life's-blast,
Delight mid the doughty.
                              Days little durable,
And all arrogance of earthen riches,
There come now no kings nor Cæsars
Nor gold-giving lords like those gone.
Howe'er in mirth most magnified,
Whoe'er lived in life most lordliest,
Drear all this excellence, delights undurable!
Waneth the watch, but the world holdeth.
Tomb hideth trouble. The blade is layed low.
Earthly glory ageth and seareth.
No man at all going the earth's gait,
But age fares against him, his face paleth,
Grey-haired he groaneth, knows gone companions,
Lordly men are to earth o'ergiven,
Nor may he then the flesh-cover, whose life ceaseth,
Nor eat the sweet nor feel the sorry,
Nor stir hand nor think in mid heart,
And though he strew the grave with gold,
His born brothers, their buried bodies
Be an unlikely treasure hoard.

ECHOES

GUIDO ORLANDO, SINGING

Befits me praise thine empery, Lady of Valour,
Past all disproving;
Thou art the flower to me—
  Nay, by Love's pallor—
Of all good loving.

Worthy to reap men's praises
Is he who'd gaze upon
  Truth's mazes.
In like commend is he,
Who, loving fixedly,
Love so refineth,

Till thou alone art she
  In whom love's vested;
As branch hath fairest flower
  Where fruit's suggested.

II *

Thou keep'st thy rose-leaf
Till the rose-time will be over,
Think'st thou that Death will kiss thee?
Think'st thou that the Dark House
  Will find thee such a lover
As I? Will the new roses miss thee?

Prefer my cloak unto the cloak of dust
  'Neath which the last year lies,
For thou shouldst more mistrust
  Time than my eyes.

This great joy comes to me,
  To me observing
How swiftly thou hast power
  To pay my serving.

* Asclepiades, Julianus Ægyptus.

AN IMMORALITY

Sing we for love and idleness,
Naught else is worth the having.

Though I have been in many a land,
There is naught else in living.

And I would rather have my sweet,
Though rose-leaves die of grieving,

Than do high deeds in Hungary
To pass all men's believing.

DIEU! QU'IL LA FAIT

From Charles D'Orleans
For music

God! that mad'st her well regard her,
How she is so fair and bonny;
For the great charms that are upon her
Ready are all folk to reward her.

Who could part him from her borders
When spells are alway renewed on her?
God! that mad'st her well regard her,
How she is so fair and bonny.

From here to there to the sea's border,
Dame nor damsel there's not any
Hath of perfect charms so many.
Thoughts of her are of dream's order:
God! that mad'st her well regard her.

Δῶρια

Be in me as the eternal moods
            of the bleak wind, and not
      As transient things are—
            gaiety of flowers.
Have me in the strong loneliness
            of sunless cliffs
And of grey waters.
            Let the gods speak softly of us
In days hereafter,
            The shadowy flowers of Orcus
Remember Thee.

THE NEEDLE

Come, or the stellar tide will slip away.
Eastward avoid the hour of its decline,
Now! for the needle trembles in my soul!

Here have we had our vantage, the good hour.
Here we have had our day, your day and mine.
Come now, before this power
That bears us up, shall turn against the pole.

Mock not the flood of stars, the thing's to be.
O Love, come now, this land turns evil slowly.
The waves bore in, soon will they bear away.

The treasure is ours, make we fast land with it.
Move we and take the tide, with its next favour,
Abide
Under some neutral force
Until this course turneth aside.

SUB MARE

It is, and is not, I am sane enough,
Since you have come this place has hovered round me,
This fabrication built of autumn roses,
Then there's a goldish colour, different.

And one gropes in these things as delicate
Algæ reach up and out, beneath
Pale slow green surgings of the underwave,
'Mid these things older than the names they have,
These things that are familiars of the god.

PLUNGE

I would bathe myself in strangeness:
These comforts heaped upon me, smother me!
I burn, I scald so for the new,
New friends, new faces,
Places!
Oh to be out of this,
This that is all I wanted
          —save the new.
And you,
Love, you the much, the more desired!
Do I not loathe all walls, streets, stones,
All mire, mist, all fog,
All ways of traffic?
You, I would have flow over me like water,
Oh, but far out of this!
Grass, and low fields, and hills,
And sun,
Oh, sun enough!
Out and alone, among some
Alien people!

A VIRGINAL

No, no! Go from me. I have left her lately.
I will not spoil my sheath with lesser brightness,
For my surrounding air has a new lightness;
Slight are her arms, yet they have bound me straitly
And left me cloaked as with a gauze of æther;
As with sweet leaves; as with a subtle clearness.
Oh, I have picked up magic in her nearness
To sheathe me half in half the things that sheathe her.

No, no! Go from me. I have still the flavour,
Soft as spring wind that's come from birchen bowers.
Green come the shoots, aye April in the branches,
As winter's wound with her sleight hand she staunches,
Hath of the trees a likeness of the savour:
As white their bark, so white this lady's hours.

PAN IS DEAD

Pan is dead. Great Pan is dead.
Ah! bow your heads, ye maidens all,
And weave ye him his coronal.

     There is no summer in the leaves,
And withered are the sedges;
     How shall we weave a coronal,
Or gather floral pledges?

That I may not say, Ladies.
Death was ever a churl.
That I may not say, Ladies.
How should he show a reason,
That he has taken our Lord away
Upon such hollow season?

THE PICTURE *

The eyes of this dead lady speak to me,
For here was love, was not to be drowned out,
And here desire, not to be kissed away.

The eyes of this dead lady speak to me.

* "Venus Reclining," by Jacopo del Sellaio (1442–93).

OF JACOPO DEL SELLAIO

This man knew out the secret ways of love,
No man could paint such things who did not know.

And now she's gone, who was his Cyprian,
And you are here, who are "The Isles" to me.

And here's the thing that lasts the whole thing out:
The eyes of this dead lady speak to me.

THE RETURN

See, they return; ah, see the tentative
    Movements, and the slow feet,
    The trouble in the pace and the uncertain
    Wavering!

See, they return, one, and by one,
With fear, as half-awakened;
As if the snow should hesitate
And murmur in the wind,
              and half turn back;
These were the "Wing'd-with-Awe,"
          Inviolable.

Gods of the wingèd shoe!
With them the silver hounds,
          sniffing the trace of air!

Haie! Haie!
    These were the swift to harry;
    These the keen-scented;
    These were the souls of blood.

    Slow on the leash,
          pallid the leash-men!

EFFECTS OF MUSIC
UPON A COMPANY OF PEOPLE

DEUX MOUVEMENTS
  1. *Temple qui fut.*
  2. *Poissons d'or.*

1

A soul curls back,
    Their souls like petals,
    Thin, long, spiral,
Like those of a chrysanthemum curl
Smoke-like up and back from the
Vavicel, the calyx,
Pale green, pale gold, transparent,
Green of plasma, rose-white,
Spirate like smoke,
Curled,
Vibrating,
Slowly, waving slowly.
O Flower animate!
O calyx!
O crowd of foolish people!

2

The petals!
On the tip of each the figure
Delicate.
See, they dance, step to step.
Flora to festival,
Twine, bend, bow,
Frolic involve ye.
Woven the step,
Woven the tread, the moving.
Ribands they move,
Wave, bow to the centre.
Pause, rise, deepen in colour,
And fold in drowsily.

II

Breast high, floating and welling
　　Their soul, moving beneath the satin,
　　Plied the gold threads,
Pushed at the gauze above it.
The notes beat upon this,
Beat and indented it;
Rain dropped and came and fell upon this,
Hail and snow,
My sight gone in the flurry!

And then across the white silken,
Bellied up, as a sail bellies to the wind,
Over the fluid tenuous, diaphanous,
Over this curled a wave, greenish,
Mounted and overwhelmed it.
This membrane floating above,
And bellied out by the up-pressing soul.

Then came a mer-host,
And after them legion of Romans,
The usual, dull, theatrical!

UNCOLLECTED MISCELLANEOUS POEMS
1902–1912

EZRA ON THE STRIKE

Wal, Thanksgivin' do be comin' round.
With the price of turkeys on the bound,
And coal, by gum! Thet were just found,
    Is surely gettin' cheaper.

The winds will soon begin to howl,
And winter, in its yearly growl,
Across the medders begin to prowl,
    And Jack Frost gettin' deeper.

By shucks! It seems to me,
That you and I orter be
Thankful, that our Ted could see
    A way to operate it.

I sez to Mandy, sure, sez I,
I'll bet thet air patch o' rye
Thet he'll squash 'em by-and-by,
    And he did, by cricket!

No use talkin', he's the man—
One of the best thet ever ran,
Fer didn't I turn Republican
    One o' the fust?

I 'lowed as how he'd beat the rest,
But old Si Perkins, he hemmed and guessed,
And sed as how it wuzn't best
    To meddle with the trust.

Now Pattison, he's gone up the flue,
And Coler, he kinder got there, tew,
So Si, put thet in your cud to chew,
    And give us all a rest.

Now thet I've had my little say
I wish you all a big Thanksgivin' day,
While I plod on to town with hay,
    And enjoy it best.

[*Jenkintown Times-Chronicle*, Jenkintown, Pa., Nov. 8, 1902]

A DAWN SONG

God hath put me here
In earth's goodly sphere
    To sing the joy of the day,
A strong glad song,
If the road be long,
    To my fellows in the way.

So I make my song of the good glad light
    That falls from the gate of the sun,
And the clear cool wind that bloweth good
    To my brother Everyone.

[*Munsey's Magazine*, December, 1906]

TO THE RAPHAELITE LATINISTS

By Weston Llewmys

Ye fellowship that sing the woods and spring,
    Poets of joy that sing the day's delight,
    Poets of youth that 'neath the aisles of night
Your flowers and sighs against the lintels fling;

Who rose and myrtle in your garlands bring
    To marble altars, though their gods took flight
    Long ere your dream-shot eyes drank summer light
And wine of old time myth and vintaging,

Take of our praise one cup, though thin the wine
    That Bacchus may not bless nor Pan outpour:
Though reed pipe and the lyre be names upon
The wind, and moon-lit dreams be quite out-gone
    From ways we tread, one cup to names ye bore,
One wreath from ashes of your songs we twine!

[Book News Monthly, January, 1908]

IN EPITAPHIUM

Write me when this geste, our life is done:
"He tired of fame before the fame was won."

[The Book of the Poets' Club, 1909]

THERSITES: ON THE SURVIVING ZEUS

(With apologies to all the rhetorical odists)

I

Immortal Ennui, that hath driven men
To mightier deeds and actions than e'er Love
With all his comfit kisses brought to be,
Thee only of the gods out-tiring Time,
That weariest man to glory ere the grave,
Thee do we laud within thy greyest courts!
O thou unpraisèd one, attend our praise!

II

Great Love hath turned him back but never thou,
O steely champion, hast let slip the rein.
Great deeds were thine in Rome and Macedon
When small gods gleaned the stubble of man's praise,
And silent thou alone didst know their birth.
Revealèd wast to none but thine elect
Who trod the chaff of earth's death-dusty crowns.

III

Immortal Ennui that hath saved the world
From dry contagion of man's great dull books,
O Wisdom's self that stillest wisdom's voice,
The frank Apollo never stole thy sheep,
No song hath lured thee from thy granite throne.
There is no bourne to thine insistency,
No power to turn the sword of thy disdain.

IV

All deeds are dust and song is less than deed
Thou dost beget such hunger in the soul.
To mightier conquests and to wars more vain
The sands of men are driven by thy breath;
Thine is the high emprise [of] lordly lays.
O thou inspiring Might, drink deep this praise,
Ere our great boredom pass its several ways!

[*The English Review*, April, 1910]

THE FAULT OF IT

"Some may have blamed you—"

Some may have blamed us that we cease to speak
Of things we spoke of in our verses early,
Saying: a lovely voice is such and such;
Saying: that lady's eyes were sad last week,
Wherein the world's whole joy is born and dies;
Saying: she hath this way or that, this much
Of grace, this little misericorde;
Ask us no further word;
If we were proud, then proud to be so wise
Ask us no more of all the things ye heard;
We may not speak of them, they touch us nearly.

[*Forum*, N. Y., July, 1911]

FOR A BEERY VOICE

Why should we worry about to-morrow,
When we may all be dead and gone?
Haro! Haro!
        Ha-a-ah-rro!
There'll come better men
Who will do, will they not?
The noble things that we forgot.
If there come worse,
            what better thing
Than to leave them the curse of our ill-doing!
Haro! Haro!
        Ha-ah-ah-rro!

[*Poetry Review*, February, 1912]

L'INVITATION

Go from me. I am one of those who spoil
And leave fair souls less fair for knowing them;
Go from me, I bring light that blindeth men
So that they stagger.
           It doth ill become me.
Go from me. I am life the tawdry one,
I am the spring and autumn.
              Ah the drear
Hail that hath bent the corn!
           The ruined gold!

[*Poetry Review*, February, 1912]

EPILOGUE

(To my five books containing mediaeval studies, experiments and translations)

I bring you the spoils, my nation,
I, who went out in exile,
 Am returned to thee with gifts.

I, who have laboured long in the tombs,
 Am come back therefrom with riches.

Behold my spices and robes, my nation,
My gifts of Tyre.

Here are my rimes of the south;
Here are strange fashions of music;
Here is my knowledge.

Behold, I am come with patterns;
Behold, I return with devices,
Cunning the craft, cunning the work, the fashion.

[Composed 1912. *Collected Shorter Poems*, 1968]

POEMS WITHDRAWN FROM *CANZONI*

LEVIORA

AGAINST FORM

Whether my Lady will to hear of me
The unrimed speech wherein the heart is heard,
Or whether she prefer to the perfumed word
And powdered cheek of masking irony?
Decorous dance steps ape simplicity,
The well-groomed sonnet is to truth preferred;
Let us be all things so we're not absurd,
Dabble with forms and damn the verity.
Bardlets and bardkins, I do bite my thumb.
Corset the muse and "directoire" her grace,
Marcel the elf-looks of *sa chevelure,*
Enamel Melpomene's too sun-kissed face
And then to have your fame forged doubly sure
Let taste rule all and bid the heart be dumb.

II

HIC JACET

When we be buried in anthologies,
Subjective egoists, objective makers
Tied cheek by jowl, the true and false partakers
Of semi-fame, and drear eternities
Warmed by no fire save scholastic comment,
Will those among us who have pleased ourselves
Not sit more snugly than the crabbed elves
Who made the work a trade, as if 'twere so meant?
And when the eyes we sing to are grown dim,
Think you we fellows who have loved our loving
Think you that we, who for their sake we've sung to,
Have jammed our words within the sonnet's rim
And for love's sake set all our lines a-moving,
Think you we'll care what shelf the tomes are flung to?

IV

TO MY VERY DEAR FRIEND—REMONSTRATING
FOR HIS ESSAY UPON "MIGHTY MOUTHS"

Deaf . . . dericus, deaf . . . ingides,
Thou passest Midas, if the truth be told,

I mean in hearing and in manifold
Bombastic statement of unverities.
Leave, Friend, ah leave such wordy fields as these,
Thou deck'st poor plaster with thin leaves of gold,
And then thou chokest e'en as Midas old,
Whose fated touch begat such bright disease.

Disturb not high Olympus with the claims
Of this bemotlied mimic of the great,
Priapus hides him 'neath Jehova's coat.
Some musty corner in the tomb of fame
Where thou and —— —— shall hold future state
Would better fit this "Mouth" whom thou dost note.

TO HULME (T. E.) AND FITZGERALD (A CERTAIN)

Is there for feckless poverty
That grins at ye for a' that!
A hired slave to none am I,
But underfed for a' that;
For a' that and a' that;
The tails I shun and a' that,
My name but mocks the guinea stamp,
And Pound's dead broke for a' that.

Although my linen still is clean,
My socks fine silk and a' that,
Although I dine and drink good wine—
Say, twice a week, and a' that;
For a' that and a' that,
My tinsel show and a' that,
These breeks 'll no last many weeks
'Gainst wear and tear and a' that.

Ye see this birkie ca'ed a bard,
Wi' cryptic eyes and a' that,

Aesthetic phrases by the yard;
It's but E. P. for a' that,
For a' that and a' that,
My verses, books and a' that,
The man of independent means
He looks and laughs at a' that.

One man will make a novelette
And sell the same and a' that.
For verse nae man can siller get,
Nae editor maun fa' that
For a' that and a' that,
Their royalties and a' that,
Wi' time to loaf and will to write
I'll stick to rhyme for a' that.

And ye may praise or gang your ways
Wi' pity, sneers and a' that,
I know my trade and God has made
Some men to rhyme and a' that,
I maun gang on for a' that
Wi' verse to verse until the hearse
Carts off me wame and a' that.

REDONDILLAS, OR SOMETHING OF THAT SORT

I sing the gaudy to-day and cosmopolite civilization
Of my hatred of crudities, of my weariness of banalities,
I sing of the ways that I love, of Beauty and delicate savours.

No man may pass beyond
        the nets of good and evil
For joy's in deepest hell
        and in high heaven,
About the very ports
        are subtle devils.

I would sing of exquisite sights,
          of the murmur of Garda;
I would sing of the amber lights,
          or of how Desenzano
Lies like a topaz chain
          upon the throat of the waters.

I sing of natural forces
          I sing of refinements
I would write of the various moods
          of nuances, of subtleties.
I would sing of the hatred of dullness,
          of the search for sensation.

I would sing the American people,
          God send them some civilization;
I would sing of the nations of Europe,
          God grant them some method of cleansing
The fetid extent of their evils.
          I would sing of my love "To-morrow,"
But Yeats has written an essay,
          Why should I stop to repeat it?
I don't like this hobbledy metre
          but find it easy to write in,
I would sing to the tune of *"Mi Platz"*
          were it not for the trouble of riming,
Besides, not six men believe me
          when I sing in a beautiful measure.

I demonstrate the breadth of my vision.
          I am bored of this talk of the tariff,
I too have heard of T. Roosevelt.
          I have met with the "Common Man,"
I admit that he usually bores me,
          He is usually stupid or smug.
I praise God for a few royal fellows
          like Plarr and Fred Vance and Whiteside,
I grant them fullest indulgence
          each one for his own special queerness.

I believe in some lasting sap
        at work in the trunk of things;
I believe in a love of deeds,
        in a healthy desire for action;
I believe in double-edged thought
        in careless destruction.

I believe in some parts of Nietzsche,
        I prefer to read him in sections;
In my heart of hearts I suspect him
        of being the one modern christian;
Take notice I never have read him
        except in English selections.
I am sick of the toothless decay
        of God's word as they usually preach it;
I am sick of bad blasphemous verse
        that they sell with their carols and hymn tunes.

I would sing of the soft air
        and delight that I have in fine buildings,
Pray that God better my voice
        before you are forced to attend me.
I would turn from superficial things
        for a time, into the quiet
I would draw your minds to learn
        of sorrow in quiet,
To watch for signs and strange portents.

        · · · · ·

Delicate beauty on some sad, dull face
Not very evil, but just damned, through weakness,
Drawn down against hell's lips by some soft sense;
When you shall find such a face
        how far will your thought's lead fathom?
Oh, it's easy enough to say
        'tis this, that and the other,
But when some truth is worn smooth
        how many men really do think it?
We speak to a surfeited age,
        Grant us keen weapons for speaking.

Certain things really do matter:
          Love, and the comfort of friendship.
After we are burnt clear,
          or even deadened with knowledge;
After we have gone the whole gamut,
          exhausted our human emotions,
Still is there something greater,
          some power, some recognition,
Some bond beyond the ordinary bonds
          of passion and sentiment
And the analyzed method of novels,
          some saner and truer course
That pays us for foregoing blindness.

Whenever we dare, the angels crowd about us.
There is no end to the follies
          sprung from the full fount of weakness;
There is great virtue in strength
          even in passive resistance.
God grant us an open mind
          and the poise and balance to use it.
They tell me to "Mirror my age,"
          God pity the age if I do do it,
Perhaps I myself would prefer
          to sing of the dead and the buried:
At times I am wrapped in my dream
          of my mistress "To-morrow"
We ever live in the now
          it is better to live in than sing of.

Yet I sing of the diverse moods
          of effete modern civilization.
I sing of delicate hues
          and variations of pattern;
I sing of risorgimenti,
          of old things found that were hidden,
I sing of the senses developed,
          I reach towards perceptions scarce heeded.
If you ask me to write world prescriptions
          I write so that any can read it:

A little less Paul Verlaine,
  A good sound stave of Spinoza,
A little less of our nerves
  A little more will toward vision.

I sing of the fish and the sauce,
  I sing of the *rôti de dindon;*
I sing of delectable things that
  I scarcely ever can pay for.
I love the subtle accord
  of rimes wound over and over;
I sing of the special case,
  The truth is the individual.

Tamlin is the truest of ballads,
  There is more in heaven and earth
Than the priest and the scientists think of.
  The core in the heart of man
Is tougher than any "system."
  I sing devils, thrones and dominions
At work in the air round about us,
  Of powers ready to enter
And thrust our own being from us.
  I sing of the swift delight
Of the clear thrust and riposte in fencing,
  I sing of the fine overcoming,
I sing of the wide comprehension.
  I toast myself against the glow of life
I had a trace of mind, perhaps some heart
  Nature I loved, in her selected moods,
And art,
  perhaps a little more than need be.

I have no objection to wealth,
  the trouble is the acquisition,
It would be rather a horrible sell
  to work like a dog and not get it.
Arma, virumque cano, qui primus, etcetera, ab oris,

Even this hobbledy-hoy
          is not my own private invention.
We are the heirs of the past,
          it is asinine not to admit it.
O Virgil, from your green elysium
          see how that dactyl stubs his weary toes.

I too have been to the play-house,
          often bored with vapid inventions;
I too have taken delight
          in the maze of the Russian dancers.
I am that terrible thing,
          the product of American culture,
Or rather that product improved
          by considerable care and attention.
I am really quite modern, you know,
          despite my affecting the ancients.
I sing of the pleasure of teas
          when one finds someone brilliant to talk to.
I know this age and its works
          with some sort of moderate intelligence,
It does nothing so novel or strange
          except in the realm of mechanics.
Why should I cough my head off
          with that old gag of "Nascitur ordo"?
(The above is not strictly the truth
          I've just heard of a German named Ehrlich.
Medical science is jolted,
          we'll have to call back Fracastori
To pen a new end for "De Morbo.")
          But setting science aside
To return to me and my status;
          I'm not specifically local,
I'm more or less Europe itself,
          More or less Strauss and De Bussy.
I even admire and am
          Klimt and that horrible Zwintscher.
Shall I write it: *Admiror, sum ergo?*
          Deeds are not always first proof,

Write it thus: By their Gods ye shall know them.
The chief god in hell is convention,
        'got by that sturdy sire Stupidity
Upon pale Fear, in some most proper way.
        Where people worship a sham
There is hardly room for a devil.
        You'll find some such thing in Hen. Ibsen.
I'm sorry Dame Fashion has left him
        and prefers to imbibe him diluted
In . . . Why name our whole tribe of playwrights?
        Mistrust the good of an age
That swallows a whole code of ethics.
        Schopenhauer's a gloomy decadent
Somewhat chewed by the worms of his wisdom.
        Our mud was excreted of mind,
That mudless the mind should be clearer.
        Behold how I chivvy Lucretius,
Behold how I dabble in cosmos.
        Behold how I copy my age,
Dismissing great men with a quibble.
        I know not much save myself,
I know myself pretty completely.
        I prefer most white wine to red,
Bar only some lordly Burgundy.
        We all of us make mistakes,
Give us reasonable time to retrieve them.
        The future will probably meet
With people who know more than we do.
        There's no particular end
To this sort of a statement of being,
        no formal envoi or tornata
But perhaps a sort of a bow.
        The musician returns to the dominant.
Behold then the the that I am;
        Behold me sententious, *dégagé,*
Behold me my saeculum in parvo,
        Bergson's objective fact,
London's last foible in poets.
        I love all delicate sounds,

The purple fragrance of incense;
        I love the flaked fire of sunlight
Where it glints like red rain on the water;
        I love the quaint patterns inwoven
In Mozart, Stiebelt, Scarlatti,
        I love their quavers and closes,
The passionate moods of singing.

THE ALCHEMIST (TWO VERSIONS)

1912

THE ALCHEMIST

Chant for the Transmutation of Metals

Sail of Claustra, Aelis, Azalais,
As you move among the bright trees;
As your voices, under the larches of Paradise
Make a clear sound,
Sail of Claustra, Aelis, Azalais,
Raimona, Tibors, Berangèrë,
'Neath the dark gleam of the sky;
Under night, the peacock-throated,
Bring the saffron-coloured shell,
Bring the red gold of the maple,
Bring the light of the birch tree in autumn
Mirals, Cembelins, Audiarda,
                    Remember this fire.

Elain, Tireis, Alcmena
'Mid the silver rustling of wheat,
Agradiva, Anhes, Ardenca,
From the plum-coloured lake, in stillness,
From the molten dyes of the water
Bring the burnished nature of fire;
Briseis, Lianor, Loica,
From the wide earth and the olive,
From the poplars weeping their amber,
By the bright flame of the fishing torch
                    Remember this fire.
Midonz, with the gold of the sun, the leaf of the
          poplar, by the light of the amber,
Midonz, daughter of the sun, shaft of the tree, silver
          of the leaf, light of the yellow of the amber,
Midonz, gift of the God, gift of the light, gift of
          the amber of the sun,
                    Give light to the metal.
Anhes of Rocacoart, Ardenca, Aemelis,
From the power of grass,
From the white, alive in the seed,
From the heat of the bud,

From the copper of the leaf in autumn,
From the bronze of the maple, from the sap in the bough;
Lianor, Ioanna, Loica,
By the stir of the fin,
By the trout asleep in the gray-green of water;
Vanna, Mandetta, Viera, Alodetta, Picarda, Manuela
From the red gleam of copper,
Ysaut, Ydone, slight rustling of leaves,
Vierna, Jocelynn, daring of spirits,
By the mirror of burnished copper,
                    O Queen of Cypress,
Out of Erebus, the flat-lying breadth,
Breath that is stretched out beneath the world:
Out of Erebus, out of the flat waste of air, lying
        beneath the world;
Out of the brown leaf-brown colourless
                    Bring the imperceptible cool.
Elain, Tireis, Alcmena,
                    Quiet this metal!
Let the manes put off their terror, let them put off
        their aqueous bodies with fire.
Let them assume the milk-white bodies of agate.
Let them draw together the bones of the metal.

Selvaggia, Guiscarda, Mandetta,
                    Rain flakes of gold on the water,
Azure and flaking silver of water,
Alcyon, Phætona, Alcmena,
Pallor of silver, pale lustre of Latona,
By these, from the malevolence of the dew
                    Guard this alembic.
Elain, Tireis, Allodetta
                    Quiet this metal.

[From *Umbra* (1920), where table of contents notes: "unpublished 1912."]

THE ALCHEMIST

Sail of Claustra, Aelis, Azalais
As you move among the bright trees
As your voices, under the larches of paradise
Make a clear sound,
Sail of Claustra, Aelis, Azalais,
Raimona, Tibors, Berangèrë,
'Neath the dark gleam of the sky,
Under night, the peacock-throated,
Mirals, Cembelins, Audiarda.
Bring the red-gold leaf of the maple,
Bring colour from the birch tree in autumn,
Mirals, Cembelins, Audiarda,
Remember our fire.
Raimona, Tibors, Berangèrë,
    seek the gleam on the cup.
Raimona, Tibors, Berangèrë,
    watch over our metal.

Elain, Tireis, Alcmena,
Amid the silver rustling of wheat
Move with a light tread.
Bring sound in metal
Elain, Tireis, Alcmena,
    think of our longing.

Agradiva, Anhes, Ardenca,
From the plum-coloured lake in stillness,
From the molten dyes of the water
    Bring the burnished nature of fire
Agradiva, Anhes, Ardenca,
    watch over our lembic.

Briseis, Lianor, Loica,
From the wide earth and the olive,
From the poplars weeping their amber,
By the flaked rain of the sunlight
Bring body and glitter

Briseis, Lianor, Loica,
    bring these to our fire
By the flame of the fishing torch,
        Remember this fire.

Midonz, with gold of sun, the leaf of the poplar, by the
    light of the amber. Midonz, daughter of the sun, shaft of the
    tree, silver of the leaf, light of the yellow of the amber,
    Midonz, gift of the god, gift of the light, gift of the amber
    of the sun.
        Give light to the metal.
Anhes of Rocacoart, Ardenca, Aemelis
From the power of grass, from the white alive in the seed,
    from the heat of the bud, from the copper of the leaf in
    autumn, from the bronze of the maple, from the sap in the
    bough
Lianor Ioanna Loica
By the stir of the fin, by the trout asleep
    by the green grey of streams,
Vanna, Mandetta, Viera
Alodetta, Picarda, Manuela,
            From the red gleam of copper, the hand of
    our lady of cypress, matter of fire.
Ysaut, Ydone, Ysaves
            slight rustling of leaves, pure spirit of metal,
Ysaut, Ydone, Ysaure
Vierna, Jocelyn, Miquela
    daring of spirits
The mirrour of burnished copper, o queen of Cypress.

Out of Erebus, the flat-lying breadth,
The breath that is stretched beneath the world
Out of Erebus, out of the flat waste of air lying
Beneath the world, out of the brown leaf-coloured colourless
Bring the imperceptible cool
Elain Tireis Alcmena
        quiet this metal.
Let the manes put off their terror, let them put off
    their aqueous bodies, with fire, let them assume the
    milkwhite bodies of agate,

           let them draw together the bones of the metal
Selvaggia, Guiscarda, Mandetta
                    rain flakes gold on the water.
Rain that is entombed in the earth, rain under sun,
As the rain of fire has fallen, a hail of suns out of night.

Azure and flaking silver of water, gold in the sea.
Out of ichor of sea, out of passion of water, gold in the blood,
Naumaka
        blue over desert, voices of sand
Mahaut, Cembelins, Audiart, Mirals, Alcmena, Maent,
Raimona, Tibors, Berangèrë,
        Alcyon, Mnasidika,
Plum-coloured lake, Azemar, Bresiliada,
Flame of the fisherman's torch, gleam of many scales,
        manes coming through darkness
Doria, Phaetona, Alença
        pallor of silver, pale lustre of Latona
                from the ever-flowing, from the
        malevolence of the dew
                guard this alembic
        Animis
                guard this alembic.
        Silver crashing of wheat,   .
Mahaut, Cembelins, Esmengards
                        crashing of cymbals
        Allodetta, Picarda, Biatritz de Dia.
        Dark edge of the cloud.

[From typescript and manuscripts in the Pound Archive]

POEMS FROM
THE SAN TROVASO NOTEBOOK

SAN VIO. JUNE

Old powers rise and do return to me
Grace to thy bounty, O Venetian sun.
Weary I came to thee, my romery
A cloth of day-strands raveled and ill-spun,
My soul a swimmer weary of the sea,
The shore a desert place with flowers none.

Old powers rise and do return to me.
The strife of waves, their lusty harmony
A thundered thorough bass the rocks upon,
Makes strong forgotten chanteys, and anon
My heart's loud-shouted burden proves to thee
Old powers risen have returned to me.

June 22

ROUNDEL FOR ARMS

All blood and body for the sun's delight,
Such be the forms, that in my song bid spring,
Should lead my lyric where the ways be dight
With flowers fit for any garlanding
And bid the lustre of our arms be bright
Who do our chaunting 'gainst the "Lord Gloom" fling.

All blood and body for the sun's delight,
I bid ye stand, my words, and in the fight
Bear ye as men and let your glaive-strokes ring
Basnet on falchion 'till the chorusing
Proclaim your triumph and ye stand aright,
All blood and body for the sun's delight.

Cino. June.

ROUNDEL

After Joachim du Bellay

I come unto thee thru the hidden ways,
Soul of my soul, whose beauty quivereth
Within her eyes to whom my former days
As wined libation poured I, while my breath
Strove to her homage in unskillful lays
And bade my heart make his high vaunt 'gainst death.

I come unto thee thru the hidden ways
Who art the soul of beauty, and whose praise
Or color, or light, or song championeth,
And of whom Time as but an herald saith,
"Trust tho thou sense not, spite of my delays,
Her whom I bring thee thru the hidden ways."

Cino. June

234

SONNET OF THE AUGUST CALM

When Summer hath her noon, it likes me lie
Somewhile quite parted from the stream of things,
Watching alone the clouds' high wanderings,
As free as they are in some wind-free sky,

While naught but weirds of dream as clouds glide by
Or come as faint blown wind across the strings
Of this odd lute of mine imaginings
And make it whisper me quaint runes and high.

In such a mood have I such strange sooth seen
And shapes of wonder and of beauty's realm
Such habitants, that time's uncertainty
Upwells within me and doth nigh o'erwhelm
My body's life, until Truth dawns to me
That where the treasure is the heart hath been.

S. Trovaso. June

TO YSOLT. FOR PARDON.

My songs remade that I send greet the world
Thou knowest as at first they came to me,
Freighted with fragrance of thyself and furled
In stumbling words that yet us seemed to be
True music, sith thy heart and mine empurled
Their outer sense with inner subtlety.

My songs remade that I send greet the world
Me seem as red leaves of the Autumn whirled
Out thru the dust-grey ways, that dearer we,
As green bough-banners, held more lovingly
With simpler color than these turn-coats hurled,
As songs remade sent forth to greet the world.

?San Trovaso

FOR YSOLT. THE TRIAD OF DAWN.

Phila. 07.
August. or Sept.

[I]

Unto her wonderful, the night's own might
That is the spirit of the gloom and keys
These seven dol'rous lays of mine ill ease
With freight of malice, venomous of blight,
Have born out all my grief upon the night.
Lo, with the dawn there whirreth mid the trees
Thru foliate sunlight madrigal of bees
Crying to Myop "See God's earth aright."

Wherefor I turn me now from all her splendor
That is all mystery and portent strange,
And all the lure of pain such might should lend her
Is broken night before the law of change
Nor secret lore availeth to defend her
When dawn is up and takes the sky his range.

[II]

May hap my words are dark, as were the lays
That shew me bitter on a vanquished field.
But now, sith sunlight for a brand I wield
Behoov'th me sing thru unencumbered ways.
Black gloom I cried to open earth's dispraise
And praised her singing where the mock'ry pealed
In tearful bell-note for all wounds ill healed,
And wept for Truth's sake Truth's o'er-clouded days.

Because she sang me might amid the gloom
I cried unto her when the gloom's returning
Had dammed my soul unto such bitter tomb
I saw him not for might of all my yearning
And fought against my visions narrow room
Till heat of words set all my heart a-burning.

[III]

If for so small a flame I praise the light
Shall I be tacit of munificence,
Hold back wing'd words from running throat-ways whence
These low-bowed pilgrims won to broader sight
And from the barren hold, inchoate flight
Foreboded. Sun-child shall my alms dispense
Pot-scrapings solely of gloom's opulence
Or shall bard fiat and all things be bright.

I cry no less *her* grace who sing to thee
For wonder of the chords her soul unfoldeth.
I own her glory in no less degree
And yet some truth that only thine heart holdeth
And reacheth toward my knowing lovlily
Bids me cry, sun, the soul of earth beholdeth.

PIAZZA SAN MARCO.

June.

[I]
Master Will, so cussed human,
Careless-clouted god o' speech,
Is there twist o' man or woman
Too well-hidden for thy reach?

Diadems and broken roses,
Wind and Tritons loud at horn,
Sack-stains half thy screed discloses,
Th' other half doth hold the morn.

[II]
Some comfort 'tis to catch Will Shaxpeer stealing.
All bards are thieves save Villon, master thief,
Who pilfered naught but wine and then, wide reeling,
Lilted his heart out, Ballad-Lord in chief.
(True to his song's good, spit the fate hands dealing,
With lips the bolder for a soul-hid grief.)

[III—AFTER SHAKESPEARE'S SONNET]
XCVIII
When proud-pied April leadeth in his train
And yellow crocus quick'neth to the breath
Of Zephyr fleeting from the sun-shot rain,
Then seek I her whom mine heart honoureth.
She is a woodland sprite and suzerain
Of every power that flouteth wintry death.

When proud-pied April leadeth in his train
And freeth all the earth from cold's mort-main,
Then with her fairness mine heart journeyeth
Thru bourgeon wood-ways wherein tourneyeth
Earth's might of laughter 'gainst all laughter slain
Ere proud-pied April led in feat his train.

LOTUS-BLOOM

What tho the lotus bloom
    This our Fenicé
Doth hold its strong enchantment
        oer my soul
What tho the lotus of heaven
     oer this our Fenicé
   Shedeth a stole,
Shedeth a stole of white light
        that cloud-broken
Maketh a dream "the Saluté"
       white token
Of grace of old graunted
       In this our Fenicé

Two candles offerèd unto that Queen
That for new dreaming "coelum regnit
Et regnet in semper" O Matri Dei,
Yea these twain towers, to thee?
     And yet the older queen?

Upon the hills of Greece, I ween,
Her diadem, her arc, hath been
Of older Times than thine the altar lamp.
She lighteth thy candles
     O Matri Dei
Yea, by her light are they brightened
    that give thee their praise.

"The song of the Lotus of Kumi!"
      Yea the old lays
That to Isis they chaunted of eld
Praisèd thy lamp in the night.

Regina sub quale?

What tho the lotus-bloom
                    This our Fenicé
Doth hold its strong enchauntment
                    Oer my soul
What tho the lotus of heaven
                    Oer this our Fenicé
          Looseth her stole!

Unto three queens mine homage
Unto thine eyes my heart

"For tis our wont to dream
                    of distant friends
And half-forgotten Times."

Unto three queens mine homage
Unto thine eyes my heart
Sendeth old dreams of the spring time.
Yea of wood-ways my rime
Found thee and flowers in, and of all streams
That sang low burthen, and of roses
That lost their dew-bowed petals
                    for the dreams
We scattered o'er them passing by.
What tho the lotus-bloom
                    This our Fenicé
Doth hold its strong enchantment
                    Oer my soul
Shall stronger wizardry
                    than her's not roll
The might of old dreams toward me
                    or the scroll
Of old imaginings not ope?

Once I have seen the law-scrolls bound
Upon two staves that bear strange names
And saw there holy things opened and read
                    while round

The synagogue, beneath quaint flames
Of high-hung lamps of silver, gowned
      In older fashion than our own
There went processional levite and priest.

              IV

E'en as the coil of the Law between its staves
So is this coil "the Saluté" where the waves,
The low rising flow of Giudecca,
                run in behind it.
And e'en as such staves
              the twin pillars
Bear it between them.
          So of the older law
Shall I not read?
Grace to who holds my screed
       Regina sub quale?

                       S. Vio. June.

FOR A PLAY.

      (Maeterlinck)

Personality—amour
        brings me to death,

My lady Willow-wisp
        that brings me to light
(a wandered forest gleam that fades)
leaving me to see the rocks turn
as if sans her connection
        and then the sun,
The sea sapphire, the grass emerald
and the white-blue above.

                 S. Vio. June

THE RUNE

O heart o' me,
Heart o' all that is true in me,
Beat again.

O Love o' me,
Love out of all that is true in me,
Rise again.

Gib[raltar].   March

NARCOTIC ALCOHOL

They call thee lecherous.
Speak! Canst thou be treacherous?
That art so fair?
The others have failed me, all.
Unto my call
Only are thy white hands
Outstretched. I know no bands.
They prate of thy commands,
Thy sting, thy lure.

Of these one thing. I know
Naught of thy gall, thy pain,
Only to me, heart-slain,
Head-tortured, wracked of the endless strain,
Thy peace, thy rest.
Surely this thing is best,

———————

    To sleep and dream
Only thy peace, thy calm.

Granada or after   —08—

BLAZED *

That they that have not been
       shall dream new dreams of this
And ye familiar wanderers
       grew warm with memory of how
Rich-glowed as Burgundy
Was this fair spot most sweet
          at such a tide
Or were the roses by the palace wall
Most sweet for March
       or for Mid-summer's call
At such or such a place along the way
Or of what eyes ye kissed at such a spot
Or "would have kissed had not

          ————————————

      eh. some trifle intervened."

  * Term as in forestry.

FOR THE TRIUMPH OF THE ARTS

> And what are the Arts?
> The Protagonist, "The Truths that speak
> with Beauty for a tongue."
>
> And (to the protagonist) who
> art thou?
> "Write me then Mammon
> his arch enemy."
>
> S. Trovaso   July

Jacques Chardinel—Of the Albigenses

I

Ye that a thousand earth-spins
            hence shall read these lines
And marvel that they gave me bitter bread,
Ye that a thousand years of dreamers dead
Have thrown between you and this time of mine
And dare to marvel that they let me starve,
Take mine own truth that to your teeth I tell
That they that speak the truth get your disdeign
And stones and die about your gates
            even as we
That bore truth's lamp did from your forebears fare.
Earth casts out truth and did and will
Until that all-consuming flame,
            our God of Truth,
Shall slay the earth y-drowned
            in 'ts molten gold.

II

O ye my brothers of the flame that after fare,
Count not your dying bitter gueredon,
But as ye keep the flame and die thereon
Cry out your triumph to th'encircling stars.

We die and live because our truth goes on.
They die and rot nor do their tombs remain.

Be glad your chançon, tho your
                    tongues grow faint
And give thy cloak to beauty, tho the cold
Of all the world that seeks to slay
Beauty, shall bitter be
                    To bear thy life away.

Triumph, and Triumph
                    for the arts fail not
While yet our blood
                    shall bid the arts withstay
Hate and the cold and wrath
                    wherewith the world would slay
Beauty, that being Truth doth all
                    the world
Accuse of all world's shame and
                    worldly littleness.

Io Triumphe, till the sun with us
Shall die for one last time
                    entombed in gold.

                (Simon's soldiers stop his mouth with a spear.)

ALMA SOL VENEZIAE

(Baritone)

Thou that hast given me back
      Strength for the journey,
Thou that hast given me back
      Heart for the Tourney,

O Sun venezian,
      Thou that thru all my veins
Hast bid the life-blood run,
Thou that hast called my soul
      From out the far crevices,
Yea, the far dark crevices
      And caves of ill-fearing,

            Alma tu sole!
Cold, ah a-cold
      Was my soul in the caves
      Of ill-fearing.

                              S. Vio.

FRAGMENT TO W. C. W.'S ROMANCE

Oh Hale green song,
O Song as water flowing,
That cooleth all my soul
And freeth me, from shapes
Of dread,
            and every gloom
From out the dark
That threatneth me and leereth
From the walls of this my consciousness
And hisseth mutterings against my heart.

O stream soft-flowing of thy good content
That healeth, blesseth and is soft unto
My forehead twitch-strained
                    and mine eyes that tire.
O thou soft-breathèd song of sweet content,
Of fields and flowers and hale greenery,
Thou calm of friendliness that be my friend
As mead unto my lips in honied flow
That soothes, that healeth all this heart o' me.

This factious striver 'gainst the ways o' men,
This sore rent prophet in the streets of guile,
This pilgrim weary in an age wherein
The truth lies panting in the ways of gain.
O blessedness of calm and of content,
O hale green song that this my
                    friend hath sent
As wind sea-strong of salt
            upon my lips to be
An after-dream-thing of
                old minstrelsy.
O take my thanking, for to give
                thee praise
Were but a base thing sith
            my heart doth raise
Its banners greeting thee as friend,
                tho to the gaze
Of many thou shalt stand
                forth and be
A song, a romance—
            a celebrity.

                N. J.—March

[FRAGMENTI]

O tender-heartedness right bitter grown
Because they knew thee not in all the world
Nor would, that gentleness thou hast to give.

       . . . . .

And are chevaliers in the court of Him
Who reigneth ever where the stars grow dim
Beyond our sight.

       . . . . .

Marble smooth by flowing waters grown.

[IN THAT COUNTRY]

Looking upon my Venice and the stars
There stood one by me and his long cool hands
On mine were layed as in the times before.

Wherefor this question rose which I set forth.

Whether 'twere better, forge of thine own soul
Thy hand-wrought image in the things of earth,
Or were it better in a gentler fashion
Weighing man's song by other signs of worth
To hover astral o'er some other soul
And breathe upon it thine own outpouring passion
Of how this line were wrought or how from chaos
The God outwrought the sprinkled dust of stars
Or say what blending
Of hue on hue on hue would make the ending
Of such a sketch or such show how the night
Is cavernous and dark and how deep hollows
Behind the veil of shade grow luminous
If eye but knew the secret there indwelling.

       . . . . .

Or sing strange runes past this my pen's faint telling,
Recondite chaunting of the ways unknown,
Of how the fields more fair are "in that country,"
And hów the Truths stand visible and whole
—Platon hath seen them thus,
                    we know who dream—

Whether 'twere better, with one's own hand to fashion
One lone man's mirroring upon the sand
Or were it better in the air to glide
From heart to heart and fill each heart with passion
To see, and make, and know what truths abide.

Una pax tibi, let the dream abide.

AUTUMNUS

To Dowson—Antistave

Lo that the wood standeth drearily!
But gaunt great banner-staves the trees
Have lost their sun-shot summer panoplies
And only the weeping pines are green,
The pines that weep for a whole world's teen.
Yet the Spring of the Soul, the Spring of the Soul
Claimeth its own in thee and me.

Lo the world waggeth wearily,
As gaunt grey shadows its people be,
Taking life's burthen drearily,
Yet each hath some hidden joy I ween,
Should each one tell where his dream hath been
The Spring of the Soul, the Spring of the Soul
Might claim more vassals than me and thee.

                                    July 13.

FRATELLO MIO, ZEPHYRUS

My wandered brother wind wild bloweth now
Driving his leaves upon a dust-smit air.
September, "proud-pied gold," that sang him fair
With green and rose tint on the maple bough
Sulks into dullard brown and doth endow
The wood-way with an tapis rich and rare,
And where King-Oak his panoply did wear
The dawn doth show him but an shorne stave now.

Me-seem'th the wood stood in its pageantry
A castle galliarded to greet its queen
That now doth bear itself but ruefully.
A grief whereof I get no bastard teen
Sith one there is doth bear the spring to me
Despite the blast that blow'th the autumn keen.

FOR E. McC.

The Rejected Stanza

Gone ere the tang of earth
Grew toothless and muttering mirth,
Gone while the wine was red to you,
Gone ere good jests were dead to you,
Gone ere the birds were sped to you,
        The birds of desire,
Gone with the spray on your eyelids,
        The spray of the broken waves,
Gone ere the loves of women
        Sought out little graves,
Little desolate graves each one.

BALLAD OF WINE SKINS

As winds thru a round smooth knot-hole
Make tune to the time of the storm,
The cry of the bard in the half-light
Is chaos bruised into form.

The skin of my wine is broken,
Is sunken and shrunken and old.
My might is the might of thistle down,
My name as a jest out-told.

Yet there cometh one in the half-light
That shieldeth a man with her hair,
And what man crouch from in his soul
The child of his heart shall bear.

I WAIT

As some pale-lidded ghost that calls
I wait secure until that other goes
Leaving thee free for thy high self of old,
Upon which soul then free, will mine beget
Such mighty fantasies as we before
Bade stand effulgent and rejoice the world.

I wait secure and waiting know I not
A bite of anger at thy littleness, nor even envy
Of that other one that bindeth thee
Within the close-hewn shroud of womanhood.

Being at peace with God and all his stars
Why should I quail the stings of nettle Time
Or fret the hour.
                    Are there canals less green
Or do the mottled colors of reflexion
Less dew their waters with mild harmony?
Is there less merriment and life withall
Amid this hoard of half-tamed brats
That rollick o'er the well-curb,
                              while one crowned
In mock of finery doth lead the rout
Half-scared at all the
                         new-found pomp
Atop of him?
                A Czar in very soul.
And if they mock the world in this their spot
Is not their jest as near to
                      wisdom as are we?

[SHALOTT]

I am the prince of dreams,
                    Lord of Shalott,
And many other things long since forgot.
Oer land & sea
I roam where it pleaseth me
And whither no man knoweth
Save the wind that bloweth   free.

BATTLE DAWN

Hail brother dawn that casteth light
        athwart the world
And comest as a man against the night.
Unsheathe the sun-blade brand and smite
All owl-winged gloom and dred outright.

      For this our phalanx is
            at one with thee
Phoibei, Phoibei, Apollo.

               S. Tr[ovaso]. July 29

FOR ITALICO BRASS

From boat to boat the bridge makes long its strand
And from death's isle they on returning way
As shadows blotted out against far cloud
Hasten for folly or with sloth delay.
When thou knowst all that these my hues strive say
Then shalt thou know the pain that eats my heart.
Some see but color and commanding sway
Of shore line, bridge line, or how are composed
The white of sheep clouds ere the wolf of storm
That lurks behind the hills
        shall snap wind's leash
And hurl tumultuous on the peace before.
But I see more.

Some as I say
See but the hues that gainst more hues laugh gay
And weave bright lyric of such interplay
As Monet claims is all the soul of art.
But I see more.

If 'tis Death's isle to North
                    shall I not know
How death's own isle doth in
                    some wise partake
Of all the reek and mystery of braggart death?
And if the hoard returns
                    Tis as one saith,
"That boasted door not every
                    way concludes."
What—if? Tis out of death we come
And not thereto as every old wive's saw
Worn toothless saith.
Tis thither thither wafts the
                    life-wind's breath.

And to the West that pregnancy
                    that bodes the storm
Unsensed of foregrounds
                    "oil upon the sea"
If here the water and the
                    tranquil folk
See not the lowered West, his threatening,
Can these things be
But play of shade and web of line to me?

When thou knowst all that these my hues strive say,
Then shalt thou know some whit the pain
That gnaws, then shalt thou
                    know some whit the strain
That spite the palate
                    eats the heart away.

Aug. 7   S. Trovaso

ENVOI

A mon bien aimé

Well have I loved ye,
        little songs of mine,
Well have I loved the
        days that saw ye born.
As frail perfections
        blown upon the wing
I bid ye "via!"
        And as unconfinèd be ye
As swallows
        winnowing the wind
—before the pale clouds
        taste the wine of morn—
While th' uncrushed
        stars still cling upon the vine.

She is a thing too frail to know
                    our life,
Its strife and torment and the changing tides.

Lo I would have her writ—on some
                    fair page—
The finest parchment and the dearest gold.

Thoughts moving
          in her eyes
as sunset color
          shadows
               on Giudecca.

The haze
          that
          doth the sun prolong.

I have felt the lithe wind
          blowing
                    under one's fingers
          sinuous.

STATEMENT OF BEING

I am a grave poetic hen
That lays poetic eggs
And to´enhance my temperament
A little quiet begs.

We make the yolk philosophy,
True beauty the albumen.
And then gum on a shell of form
To make the screed sound human.

DAS BABENZORN

Scorns have I seen but Lady Babchen's scorn
Outscorneth all the scorns that I have seen.
All ye that pass I bid my song forwarn
Lest for some dyeing of deep verdant green
That with thee in thine intellect was born
Thou catch the chance to learn what "scorn" doth mean.

Scorns have I seen but Lady Babchen's scorn
Hath all scorns scornèd leaving them forlorn
As moulting candles when the sun doth preen
His ostrich plumage in the noon's serene.
Swear not to conquer it lest thou forsworn
Return from meeting mit den Babenzorn.

POEMS FROM MISCELLANEOUS
MANUSCRIPTS

SWINBURNE: A CRITIQUE

Blazes of color intermingled,
Wondrous pattern leading nowhere,
Music without a name,
Knights that ride in a dream,
Blind as all men are blind,
Why should the music show
                    Whither they go?
I am Swinburne, ruler in mystery.
        None know the ending,
                    Blazes a-blending   in splendor
Of glory none know the meaning on,
I am he that paints the rainbow of the sunset
        And the end of all dreams,
                    Wherefor would ye know?
                    Honor the glow
Of the colors   care not wherefore   they gleam
                    All things but seem.

                    Out from Caerleon
                        Into the world unknown,
            Young knights be riding.
                    Know they love sorrow,
                    Death comes tomorrow.
            Priest of the old Gods I,
            Priest of the Gods that die,
                        Swinburne.

TO E. B. B.

(Elizabeth Barrett Browning,
Sonnets from the Portuguese)

Poor wearied singer at the gates of death
Taking thy slender sweetness from the breath
      Of the singers of old time,
With all thy sweet youth's dreaming come to naught
Save to find those same dreams fraught
With bitterness, as is to them that fare
Forth with good hope, and find despair:

When, as sun unto a leaden sea
He came, thy Poet,
Gilding each separate wave-crest
With splendor of the orient and dawn,
Making that grey soul of thine
One golden shimmer, with clear deeps
And pearled fastnesses beneath the tides.

THE SUMMONS

I can not bow to woo thee
With honey words and flower kisses
And the dew of sweet half-truths
Fallen on the grass of old quaint love-tales
Of broidered days foredone.
Nor in the murmurous twilight
May I sit below thee,
Worshiping in whispers
Tremulous as far-heard bells.
All these things have I known once
And passed
In that gay youth I had but yester-year.

And that is gone
As the shadow of the wind.
Nay, I can not woo thee thus;
But as I am ever swept upward
To the centre of all truth
So must I bear thee with me
Rapt into this great involving flame,
Calling ever from the midst thereof,
     "Follow! Follow!"
And in the glory of our meeting
Shall the power be reborn.
And together in the midst of this power
Must we, each outstriving each,
Cry eternally:
     "I come, go thou yet further."
And again, "Follow,"
For we may not tarry.

BALLAD OF THE SUN'S HUNTING

I hang from the horn of the crescent moon
    To watch the sun out-ride.
He's a-riding o' the boundries
    By creation's t'other side.

I left myself a-weeping
    For a love that would not smile.
My soul hath rode a-hunting
    With the star dogs for a while.

I hang from the horn of the crescent moon
    To watch the hunt out-ride.
There rings shrill cry and horning
    From creation's t'other side.

My soul hath caught the sun out-riding
    By creation's t'other side.
The sun hath kissed her lips out-right
    And hath my soul to bride.

Ezra Pound, Milligan Place, Crawfordsville, Ind.

QUIA AMORE LANGUEO

Tho I steal sweet words from long ago,
Tho I sing in the sun and the rain,
I bid thee come where the west winds blow
     Quia Amore langueo
And forget the world and the old world pain
     Quia Amore langueo.

Tho I can not sing with the organ's note,
Still I use the best that I know,
Tho my song were the cry of a broken rote
     Quia Amore langueo
I bid thee come where the west winds blow
In the land of the warm spring rain.

Tho I wander far in the rain and the wind
That rose-strewn land I may not find
     Quia Amore langueo
Unless you call thru the forest dim
     "Quia Amore langueo,
Come! O heart to the utmost rim
Of the worlds beyond the sea,
     Quia Amore langueo,
Bear thou thy love unto me."

Many a voice my ear hath heard
Thru the soft green shadow o' pine
     Quia Amore langueo
For false loves know many a luring word
Ere one hath won unto thine,
Ere one hath come where the west winds blow
     Quia Amore langueo
To the land of the sweet spring rain.

    Ezra Pound, Crawfordsville, Ind.

CAPILUPUS SENDS GREETING TO GROTUS *

Mantua 1500

To Giles Grotus, *vir amplissimus,*
Man to the full, who'll take
My saying for what it's worth
And for its directness. Straight
From the shoulder will I speak
And strike. For know ye
I care no more for the tumble of an ictus
Or the tinkle of a rime
Than thou dost for the color
Of the paper my brief words
Be printed on,
So to God's glory they be strong,
With all a man's good feeling
And contempt of sneers.
And know ye that I will not bend
To rime yoke nor to time yoke,
Nor will I bow to Baal
Nor weak convention
That the crawlers think is law.
An ye read me not for my hard thinking
And strong feeling, and for my love of beauty
That is strong above them all
(and is as hill-dew to the grass
and as starlight to the waters of the ford)
      Then read me not.
Thou Grotus lovest flowers
And this beauty that I follow as the stars the sun;
Therefor wilt thou read me.
Thou too canst think and feel and therefor
Wilt thou read me, that thou mayst know
What I think and feel
And thereby add to thy knowledge of mankind

---

* Capilupus, latin poet of early renaissance. His "Song to the night" is among [the] masterpieces [of] late latin. Grotus imaginary. This is accompaniment thereto, when sending same to his friend.
    Ezra Pound. Wyncote

One grain more fact and
One strain more of fancy.
Mayhap some quaintness or some odd
Crotchet of my manner'll make
Thee a´smile to keep some cold half-hour
Only half-frozen. Mayhap some half-hundred
Other half things.
Know thou to end this much,
That I do love thee and respect thee,
That I send thee first my poem
And after thee, such others as may choose
To scoff or smile or be content therewith
As may best suit their temper
Or their mood or state of being.
And lastly to such others
Whose heads are like
A store box, where Kings
And misers put their treasure,
        And God's trash,
May such find herein some fact
Or thought and put it in that
Store box head of theirs—
To keep six months and rot.
        But unto thee Grotus and them like thee
Who make each new thought and fact
A tool to make their newer thought
Or light to find new fact,
To thee God's greeting and my poem
With right good will, love and
                VALE.
There will be ever some to say
"He hath no novelty, this is of one man
And this from that old tome you know well,
On the fourth shelf third from end."
        For this, know you that I would
Make my poem, as I would make my self,
From all the best things, of all good men
And great men that go before me.
          Yet above all be myself.

The test tubes of your alchemy give me the figure
For, some fluid that you call a certain long equation,
Plus some new substance,
Is no longer the same fluid but a new,
Though all the elements thereof
Be known unto thy father's father in thine art.
Yet as ever by some new combination of old elements
Ye do seek the gold, so seek I perfection;
And as in your searching, ye find not gold
But have found and will find through coming cycles
        Many new things of old elements,
All for man's use and mayhap better for some use
And present purpose than the very gold.
        So make I rimes
Seeking ever gold, yet happy
If by chance break of syphon
Or some slip of flame
I fall on some new color
To delight the eye, as Caponlani
At his glass furnace yesteryear,
Or some new perfume, as "What's-his-name"
That's been ten years courting
Guido, for his daughter's dowry.

THE HILLS WHENCE

I will get me up unto the hills:
Unto the great bare mountains of my birth.

And the winds shall be keen upon my lips
And I will be free
                          of the damp
And twining mist of the low-land.

I will get me up unto the hills:
Unto the great bare mountains.

And I will stand me a shadow
'gainst the blue metal
          of the sky at even.

FROM CHEBAR

Before you were, America!

I did not begin with you,
I do not end with you, America.

You are the present veneer.
If my blood has flowed within you,
Are you not wrought from my people!

Oh I can see you,
I with the maps to aid me,
I can see the coast and the forest
And the corn-yellow plains and the hills,

The domed sky and the jagged,
The plainsmen and men of the cities.

I did not begin aboard "The Lion,"
I was not born at the landing.

They built you out of the woods
And my people hewed in the forest,
My people planned the rails
And devised your ways for water.

Before they found you with ships
They knew me in Warwick and Cornwall,
They knew me at Crécy and Poictiers,

     my name was aloud in the East.

Out of the old I was, I held against the Romans,
I am not afraid of the dark,
I am he who is not afraid to look in the corners.

I have seen the dawn mist
Move in the yellow grain,
I have seen the daubed purple sunset;
You may kill me, but I do not accede,
You may ignore me, you may keep me in exile,
You may assail me with negations, or you
     may keep me, a while, well hidden,
But I am after you and before you,
And above all, I do not accede.

I do not join in the facile praises,
In the ever ready cries of enthusiasms.

I demand the honesty of the forest, I am not
To be bought with lies.

I am "He who demands the perfect,"
I am he who will not be put off,

I came with the earliest comers,
I will not go till the last.

Your personal ambition is not enough,
Your personal desire for notoriety
        is insufficient.
There is only the best that matters.
Have done with the rest. Have done with
        easy contentments.
Have done with the encouragement
        of mediocre production.

I have not forgotten the birthright.
I am not content that you should be
        always a province.
The will is not enough,
The pretence is not enough,
The satisfaction-in-ignorance is insufficient.

There is no use your quoting Whitman against me,
His time is not our time, his day and hour
        were different.

The order does not end in the arts,
The order shall come and pass through them.

The state is too idle, the decrepit church is too idle,
The arts alone can transmit this.
They alone cling fast to the gods,
Even the sciences are a little below them.
They are "Those who demand the perfect,"
They are "Not afraid of the dark,"
They are after you and before you.

They have not need of smooth speeches,
There are enough who are ready to please you.

It is I, who demand our past,
And they who demand it.

It is I, who demand tomorrow,
And they who demand it.

It is we, who do not accede,
We do not please you with easy speeches.

"CHOMMODA"

"et hinsidias Arrius insidias"
                    Catullus

For two years I had observed this impeccable Mycennienne profile,
I had observed the wave-patterns in her chevelure,
At the end of that time she spoke.

I said (she was drawing the blind), and I said,
The closing regulations say you should close at 8:30;
She replied:
            "Hno heyghte o'klok."

"IT IS A SHAME"—WITH APOLOGIES
TO THE MODERN CELTIC SCHOOL

Or P'ti'cru—a Ballad

I have heard the yap of the fairy dog
                  P'ti'cru
Of the pearl white pup
                  P'ti'cru
His hide is an incandescent light
His every whisker gloweth bright
                          P'ti'cru
His yap is like the sea's soft sound
                        P'ti'cru
His grave is six feet underground
                        P'ti'cru
His whine is like a horse's bark
                    P'ti'cru
He calleth people after dark
                  P'ti'cru
To chase the wind to hullabaloo
                      P'ti'cru
My heart is filled with pain
For Blutwurst is my boozum fain
To masticate and gastricate
                    P'ti'cru
Alas his nose is underground
And his chop bones may not be found
                        P'ti'cru
Wherefor alas forsooth must I
Of counternecine hunger die
                  P'ti'cru
Alas he yappeth in the wind
P'ti'cru yappeth in the wind
He chases the chickens in the barnyard of the winds
                        P'ti'cru

In the impassioned rehash of the mystically beautiful celtic mythology, I find one touching figure neglected. My Lords: justice for the fairy dog. He came from Avalon. The olde frenche booke says one could not tell his qualities or beauty, and his color was historically as I have described it.

THE LOGICAL CONCLUSION

When earth's last thesis is copied
From the theses that went before,
When idea from fact has departed
And bare-boned factlets shall bore,
When all joy shall have fled from study
And scholarship reign supreme;
When truth shall "baaa" on the hill crests
And no one shall dare to dream;

When all the good poems have been buried
With comment annoted in full
And art shall bow down in homage
To scholarship's zinc-plated bull,
When there shall be nothing to research
But the notes of annoted notes,
And Baalam's ass shall inquire
The price of imported oats;

Then no one shall tell him the answer
For each shall know the one fact
That lies in the special ass-ignment
From which he is making his tract.
So the ass shall sigh uninstructed
While each in his separate book
Shall grind for the love of grinding
And only the devil shall look.

Against the "germanic" system of graduate study and insane specialization
in the Inanities.

Appendix
UNCOLLECTED MISCELLANEOUS POEMS
1913–1917

PAX SATURNI

Once . . . the round world brimmed with hate,
. . . . and the strong
Harried the weak. Long past, long past, praise God
In these fair, peaceful, happy days.

                                                    A Contemporary

O smooth flatterers, go over sea,
                    go to my country;
Tell her she is "Mighty among the nations"—
                    do it rhetorically!

Say there are no oppressions,
Say it is a time of peace,
Say that labor is pleasant,
Say there are no oppressions,
Speak of the American virtues:
                    And you will not lack your reward.

Say that the keepers of shops pay a fair wage to the
                    women:
Say that all men are honest and desirous of good above
                    all things:
                    You will not lack your reward.

Say that I am a traitor and a cynic,
Say that the art is well served by the ignorant pretenders:
                    You will not lack your reward.

Praise them that are praised by the many:
                    You will not lack your reward.

Call this a time of peace,
Speak well of amateur harlots,
Speak well of disguised procurers,
Speak well of shop-walkers,
Speak well of employers of women,
Speak well of exploiters,
Speak well of the men in control,

277

Speak well of popular preachers:
              You will not lack your reward.

Speak of the profundity of reviewers,
Speak of the accuracy of reporters,
Speak of the unbiased press,
Speak of the square deal as if it always occurred.
Do all this and refrain from ironic touches:
              You will not lack your reward.

Speak of the open-mindedness of scholars:
              You will not lack your reward.

Say that you love your fellow men,
O most magnanimous liar!
              You will not lack your reward.

[*Poetry*, April, 1913]

XENIA

I

THE STREET IN SOHO
Out of the overhanging gray mist
There came an ugly little man
Carrying beautiful flowers.

II
The cool fingers of science delight me;
For they are cool with sympathy,
There is nothing of fever about them.

[*Poetry*, November, 1913]

THE CHOICE

It is true that you say the gods are more use to you than fairies,
But for all that I have seen you on a high, white, noble horse,
Like some strange queen in a story.
It is odd that you should be covered with long robes and trailing
      tendrils and flowers;
It is odd that you should be changing your face and resembling
      some other woman to plague me;
It is odd that you should be hiding yourself in the cloud of
      beautiful women, who do not concern me.

And I, who follow every seed-leaf upon the wind!
      They will say that I deserve this.

[*Poetry*, November, 1913]

XENIA

IV

Come let us play with our own toys,
Come my friends, and leave the world to its muttons,
You were never more than a few,
Death is already amongst you.

V

She had a pig-shaped face, with beautiful coloring,
She wore a bright, dark-blue cloak,
Her hair was a brilliant deep orange color
So the effect was charming
As long as her head was averted.

[*Smart Set*, December, 1913]

LEGEND OF THE CHIPPEWA SPRING
AND MINNEHAHA, THE INDIAN MAIDEN

"If you press me for the legend,
For the story of this maiden,
Of this laughing Indian maiden,
Of this radiant Minnehaha
Who was won by Hiawatha,
I will answer, I will tell you
Briefly of her courtship,
And how Hiawatha won her.
She, of all Chippewa maidens,
Was the most fascinating,
And her charms were captivating;
Of the braves who sought this maiden,
And with passion almost frenzied
Led the chase and made hot battle,
Hiawatha was the bravest,
But his arrow was quite aimless,
And his game gave little heed to
Smiles of braves, or cupid's weapon.
Faint one day in early autumn,
Picking berries from the marshes,
And thirsting for a gourd of water,
She reclined upon the hillside,
Where a spring made merry laughter.
Hiawatha, from chase returning,
Saw the maiden thus reclining,
And, catching swift the inspiration,
Straightway brought the gourd of water,
Placed it to the lips so parching,
And bade her drink of 'Laughing Water,'
Scarcely had her lips been moistened,
By this fascinating nectar,
When she raised, with arms outstretching,
Bade her lover come and kiss her.
Thus it was that Hiawatha,
On the Chippewa's southern slope,
Where the fountain still is flowing,

And a city is fast growing,
Won and wed our Minnehaha,
Won and wed this beauteous maiden.
* * * * * *

Above, from happy hunting grounds,
Looking down, their watch they're keeping
On this rippling, laughing fountain,
Which gives health to all who drink it,
And with health, gives joy and gladness."

[*Chippewa County: Wisconsin Past and Present*, 1914 dated 1913]

HOMAGE TO WILFRID SCAWEN BLUNT

Because you have gone your individual gait,
Written fine verses, made mock of the world,
Swung the grand style, not made a trade of art,
Upheld Mazzini and detested institutions;

We, who are little given to respect,
Respect you, and having no better way to show it,
Bring you this stone to be some record of it.

[*The Times*, January 20, 1914]

PASTORAL

"The Greenest Growth of Maytime."—A. C. S.

The young lady opposite
Has such beautiful hands
That I sit enchanted
        While she combs her hair in décolleté.
I have no shame whatever
In watching the performance,
The bareness of her delicate
        Hands and fingers does not
        In the least embarrass me,
BUT God forbid that I should gain further acquaintance,
For her laughter frightens even the street hawker
And the alley cat dies of a migraine.

[*Blast,* June, 1914]

GNOMIC VERSES

When the roast smoked in the oven, belching out blackness,
I was bewildered and knew not what to do,
But when I was plunged in the contemplation
        Of Li Po's beautiful verses,
This thought came upon me,—
When the roast smokes, pour water upon it.

[*Blast,* July, 1915]

OUR RESPECTFUL HOMAGES
TO M. LAURENT TAILHADE

OM MANI PADME HUM
LET US ERECT A COLUMN, an epicene column,
                    To Monsieur Laurent Tailhade!
It is not fitting that we should praise him
In the modest forms of the Madrigale or the Aubade.
Let us stamp with our feet and clap hands
In praise of Monsieur Laurent Tailhade,
Whose "Poemes Aristophanesques" are
So-very-odd.
Let us erect a column and stamp with our feet
And dance a Zarabondilla and a Kordax,
Let us leap with ungainly leaps before a stage scene
By Leon Bakst.
Let us do this for the splendour of Tailhade.
            Et Dominus tecum,
                    Tailhade.

[*Blast*, July, 1915]

ET FAIM SALLIR LES LOUPS DES BOYS

I cling to the spar,
Washed with the cold salt ice
I cling to the spar—
Insidious modern waves, civilization, civilized hidden snares.
Cowardly editors threaten: "If I dare"
Say this or that, or speak my open mind,
Say that I hate my hates,
      Say that I love my friends,
Say I believe in Lewis, spit out the later Rodin,
Say that Epstein can carve in stone,
That Brzeska can use the chisel,
Or Wadsworth paint;
           Then they will have my guts;
They will cut down my wage, force me to sing their cant,
Uphold the press, and be before all a model of literary decorum.
           Merde!
Cowardly editors threaten,
Friends fall off at the pinch, the loveliest die.
That is the path of life, this is my forest.

[*Blast,* July, 1915]

LOVE-SONG TO EUNOË

Be wise:
Give me to the world,
Send me to seek adventure.

I have seen the married,
I have seen the respectably married
Sitting at their hearths:
It is very disgusting.

I have seen them stodged and swathed in contentments.
They purr with their thick stupidities.

O Love, Love,
Your eyes are too beautiful for such enactment!
Let us contrive a better fashion.

O Love, your face is too perfect,
Too capable of bearing inspection;
O Love,
Launch out your ships,
Give me once more to the tempest.

[*Smart Set*, July, 1915]

ANOTHER MAN'S WIFE

She was as pale as one
Who has just produced an abortion.

Her face was beautiful as a delicate stone
With the sculptor's dust still on it.

And yet I was glad that it was you and not I
Who had removed her from her first husband.

[*Others*, November, 1915]

POEM: ABBREVIATED FROM THE CONVERSATION OF MR. T. E. H.

Over the flat slope of St. Eloi
A wide wall of sandbags.
Night,
In the silence desultory men
Pottering over small fires, cleaning their mess-tins:
To and fro, from the lines,
Men walk as on Piccadilly,
Making paths in the dark,
Through scattered dead horses,
Over a dead Belgian's belly.

The Germans have rockets. The English have no rockets.
Behind the lines, cannon, hidden lying back miles.
Before the line, chaos:

My mind is a corridor. The minds about me are corridors.
Nothing suggests itself. There is nothing to do but keep on.

[*Catholic Anthology,* 1915]

REFLECTION

I know that what Nietzsche said is true,
And yet—
I saw the face of a little child in the street,
And it was beautiful.

[*Smart Set,* January, 1916]

TO A CITY SENDING HIM ADVERTISEMENTS

But will you do all these things?
    You, with your promises,
    You, with your claims to life,
Will you see fine things perish?
Will you always take sides with the heavy;
Will you, having got the songs you ask for,
    Choose only the worst, the coarsest?
Will you choose flattering tongues?

    Sforza . . . Baglione!
Tyrants, were flattered by one renaissance,
    And will your Demos,
Trying to match the rest, do as the rest,
The hurrying other cities,
Careless of all that's quiet,
Seeing the flare, the glitter only?

Will you let quiet men
                live and continue among you,
        Making, this one, a fane,
        This one, a building;
Or this bedevilled, casual, sluggish fellow
Do, once in a life, the single perfect poem,
        And let him go unstoned?
Are you alone? Others make talk
        and chatter about their promises,
Others have fooled me when I sought the soul.
And your white slender neighbor,
                a queen of cities,
A queen ignorant, can you outstrip her;
    Can you be you, say,
    As Pavia's Pavia
And not Milan swelling and being modern
        despite her enormous treasure?

If each Italian city is herself,
    Each with a form, light, character,
To love and hate one, and be loved and hated,
        never a blank, a wall, a nullity;

Can you, Newark, be thus,
                    setting a fashion
But little known in our land?
                    The rhetoricians
Will tell you as much. Can you achieve it?
You ask for immortality, you offer a price for it,
        a price, a prize, an honour?

You ask a life, a life's skill,
                    bent to the shackle,
                    bent to implant a soul
        in your thick commerce?
            Or the God's foot
                struck on your shoulder
                    effortless,
                being invoked, properly called,
                    invited?
I throw down his ten words,
            and we are immortal?

In all your hundreds of thousands
                    who will know this;
Who will see the God's foot,
                    who catch the glitter,
The silvery heel of Apollo;
                    who know the oblation
Accepted, heard in the lasting realm?

If your professors, mayors, judges . . . ?
                    Reader, we think not . . .
Some more loud-mouthed fellow,
                    slamming a bigger drum,
Some fellow rhyming and roaring,
        Some more obsequious back,
Will receive their purple,
                    be the town's bard,
Be ten days hailed as immortal,
        But you will die or live
        By the silvery heel of Apollo.

[*The Newark Anniversary Poems,* 1917]

NOTES

The preparation of the text and the notes for this volume has been primarily the work of Michael King, under the sponsorship of the Center for the Study of Ezra Pound and his Contemporaries in the Beinecke Rare Book and Manuscript Library of Yale University. An exception should be noted for the poems here first published from the San Trovaso Notebook, where the text has been transcribed by Donald Gallup. The editor and the introducer wish to express their gratitude to Donald Gallup for his indispensable assistance at every stage of this volume's preparation; to Mary de Rachewiltz, whose deep and intimate knowledge of her father's poetry has been a constant help and inspiration; to Peter Dzwonkoski, who ably manned the files; to Norman Holmes Pearson, whose knowledge of the relationship between H. D. and Pound was unparalleled; to James Laughlin and the Trustees of the Ezra Pound Literary Trust, for their warm encouragement of this project.

Our aim has been to collect here all the poems that Pound published, whether in book form, in periodicals, or in miscellanies, through the year 1912. This is the year that saw the appearance of *Ripostes,* a volume that marks a significant point in Pound's poetical development, for in it Pound first demonstrates his firm departure from the Victorian idiom, and his achievement of a new mode, original, colloquial, imagist. The poems in his six volumes of 1908, 1909, 1911, and 1912 have here been reprinted, including translations that appeared in these volumes; we have otherwise excluded translations from this book. (They are available in *The Translations of Ezra Pound,* with an Introduction by Hugh Kenner, 1953.) It would be desirable to have each of these six volumes complete, with their original integrity. But Pound made a practice of reprinting a good many poems from his earlier volumes in *Personae* and *Exultations,* and a few more are similarly reprinted in *Canzoni* and *Ripostes.* We have of course printed the poems only once, normally following the text of their first appearance in book form. For the convenience of readers who wish to see the original order of the poems in each volume, we have given in the notes a table of contents for *Personae* and *Exultations,* and we have noted the places where the reprinted poems appeared in *Canzoni* and *Ripostes.* A special situation exists with regard to the selections from *Canzoni* which were published seven months earlier (November 22, 1910) in *Provença* (Boston). Here we have chosen to follow the texts given in the complete volume *Canzoni* (published July, 1911), since this book was clearly planned as a unit before the selection appeared.

To these published poems we have added twenty-three hitherto unpublished poems from the San Trovaso Notebook (which Pound compiled in the year 1908), thus completing the publication of all the English poems and poetical fragments in that manuscript collection, from which a total of twenty-seven poems have previously been published in four different volumes (see discussion of this notebook below, pp. 314–16). Beyond this notebook, it is known that considerably more than a hundred of Pound's unpublished early poems exist in manuscripts (including typescripts) in various libraries, many of them in the Pound Archive at Yale. The publication of this large quantity of manuscript material must await the preparation of a separate volume. Meanwhile, we present here a selection of eleven poems from these miscellaneous manuscripts—poems that seem to have a special interest, sometimes intrinsic, sometimes with relation to Pound's career. Ten of these come from the Pound Archive, and one, "From Chebar," from the Harriet Monroe Collection of the University of Chicago Library, to which we extend our thanks for permission to publish this poem. We have also added six poems, five of them hitherto unpublished, derived from the proof sheets of Pound's volume *Canzoni* in the Humanities Research Center of the University of Texas, to which we extend our thanks for permission to reproduce these poems here. We also wish to thank the Houghton Library of Harvard University for permission to quote several passages from the original typescript of "Hilda's Book," the collection of early poems which Pound presented to Hilda Doolittle, probably in 1907. Finally, we have added in an appendix a small group of miscellaneous published verse dating from the years 1913–1917, which has not hitherto been collected, and which seems to us worthy of preservation.

All notes printed with the text of the poems are by Pound himself, except for those that are printed within square brackets.

Substantive variants in published and unpublished versions of the poems are noted; when the version is literally manuscript (i.e., handwritten), we have used the symbol "*ms.*"; when the version is done on the typewriter, we have used the symbol "*ts.*" In printing the poems from published volumes and from manuscripts, we have silently corrected obvious errors in spelling, and we have, here and there, altered the punctuation when necessary.

The history of the publication of each poem is provided through 1926, the date of the first edition of the collected shorter poems, *Personae,* with some exceptions due to later revision or special circumstances of publication. Except for the San Trovaso Notebook, no notice is made of manuscripts which exhibit no variation from published texts. For complete bibliographical information readers should consult Donald Gallup, *A Bibliography of Ezra Pound* (1963), and the supplements to that book published in *Paideuma: A Journal Devoted to Ezra Pound Scholarship.*

The following symbols are used in the notes:

A	*A Lume Spento,* Venice, 1908.
Q	*A Quinzaine for this Yule,* London, 1908.
P	*Personae,* London, 1909.
E	*Exultations,* London, 1909.
Pr	*Provença,* Boston, 1910.
C	*Canzoni,* London, 1911.
C(proofs)	*Canzoni* page proofs.
R	*Ripostes,* London, 1912.

L	*Lustra,* London, 1916.
L2	*Lustra,* New York, 1917.
U	*Umbra,* London, 1920.
P2	*Personae: the Collected Poems,* New York, 1926.
A(1958)	*A Lume Spento* 1908–1958, ed. Vanni Scheiwiller, Milan, 1958.
A(1965)	*A Lume Spento and Other Early Poems,* ed. Mary de Rachewiltz, New York, 1965.
CSP	*Collected Shorter Poems,* London, 1968.
HB	"Hilda's Book" typescript.
STN	The San Trovaso Notebook.
ms.	Manuscript (handwritten) in Pound Archive.
ts.	Typescript in Pound Archive.
⟨ ⟩	Indicates uncanceled variant in *ms.* or *ts.*

Poems are annotated for the following reasons: to provide a history of publication, to record substantive variants found in manuscripts in the Pound Archive, to record variants in cases where the poem was revised in publication after the first published version, or to note manuscript material in the Pound Archive which is directly related to the poem. The title of the annotated poem is followed by a page reference, and then by the publication history, in abbreviated form (see symbols above). Each textual variant is located by the page number and line number in this edition—with line numbers given according to lines of verse on the page (titles are excluded from the count). That is to say, 27/15 = page 27, line 15 on that page. The page and line reference is then followed by the word or phrase as it occurs in the printed text, followed by a left-face bracket (]). The variant word or phrase, as it occurs in the manuscript or other text, follows to the right of the bracket, with an editorial indication of its source. (See symbols above for abbreviations of book titles.) Uncanceled variants in the manuscripts are indicated by the use of angle brackets (⟨ ⟩). All editorial commentary in the notes is italicized, to distinguish it from text or manuscript material.

A careful comparison of the published poems has been made with the manuscript versions in the Pound Archive and in "Hilda's Book." We are aware that these collations may be only the beginning of a definitive edition, for additional manuscript versions are very likely to be uncovered. But we hope that this beginning will be of interest to readers of Pound.

M. K.
L. L. M.

GRACE BEFORE SONG (p. 7).
7/3 whose] thy *ms.*
7/4 sea] meer *ms.*
7/10] *U replaces this line with the following:* Be bold, My Songs, to seek such death as this.

LA FRAISNE (p. 9). *Reprinted: P Pr The New Poetry (1917) U P2. The Pound Archive has one manuscript and one typescript.*
9/1 For] *omitted ms.*
9/4 for] as *ms.*
9/16 mine] the *ms.*
9/19 that] and *ms.*
9/20 old] own *ms.*
9/24 And I?] *omitted ms.*
10/7] *Ts. adds before this line:* (((Here sings he:::
10/13 she was] *omitted ts.*
10/22 mid] in *ts.* amid *Pr.*

CINO (p. 10). *Reprinted: P Pr U P2. The Pound Archive has three type-scripts and one manuscript.*
Title] Ts. 2 has note: Ital. "Cino" pronounce english "Cheeno" *with ms. insertion:* C. Polnesi not to be confounded with the better known "Cino da Pistoia."
10/23] *Before this line ts. 1 adds:* loquitur
10/26] *Before this line ts. 1 adds:* (((meditating on women, what things they are, / he saith:)))
11/6 Being] We being *ts. 1.*
11/24 vagabonds] vagrants *ms.*
12/3 th' heaven o'er us] heaven air oer us *ms.* heaven oer us *ts. 2, 3.*
12/4 hath for boss thy lustre gay!] marks its bounds the luster gay *ms.* Makyth boss thy lustre gay *with ms. footnote:* "makes its boss" if clearer *ts. 2.* Makyth boss, thy lustre gay. *ts. 3.*

NA AUDIART (p. 13). *Reprinted: P Pr U P2. The Pound Archive has two typescripts and one manuscript.*
Title] Si be'm vol mal. Na Audiart *ts. 1.*
13/13 Unto Lady "Miels-de-Ben,"] Unto Miels-more-than-Ben *ts. 1. ms.*
13/23 was] is *ms.*
14/5 at] of *ts. 1.*
14/20 Churlish] Peevish *ts. 1.*
Ts. 2 is a fragment with many variants:
    Tho gainst me thine ire rise
    Audiart, Audiart.
    Well I wish of thee ⟨her⟩ plies
    Of thy ⟨her⟩ bodice shapeliness
    For its complete, it is not less Audiart, Audiart
    For any wem or faultiness

Nor doth her love a wight distress
By turns awry or wavering
And of Miels de Ben I sing
That her body fresh ⟨new⟩ and strong
straight and stately be among
The charms I call up in my song
For seemth to one with sight imbued
She did full well to bear it nude.

VILLONAUD FOR THIS YULE. (p. 15). *Reprinted: P Pr U P2.*
    15/26 hath that can] hath can give *ts.*
    15/27 are] have *ts.*

A VILLONAUD. BALLAD OF THE GIBBET (p. 16). *Reprinted: P Pr U P2.*
    16/12 mocketh his drue's disdeign] (dareth a whores) disdeign *ts.*
    16/22 And sense] And we feel *ts.*
    17/4] *Two alternate lines considered in ts.:*
        The night and birds have their frames in fee
        Whose frames have the night and its coulds for fee
    17/19 "Haulte Citee"] High City *Pr.*

MESMERISM (p. 17). *Reprinted: P Pr U P2.*

FIFINE ANSWERS (p. 18). *Reprinted: P.*
    19/13 Without our thought gives feeling] Sans thought gives us this
feeling

IN TEMPORE SENECTUTIS (p. 21). *Reprinted: P Pr Selected Poems (1928).*
    Title] In tempore senectus *A. Corrected as above P Pr.*
    22/7 He:] He saith: *P Pr. omitted ts.*
    22/8] *omitted ts.*
    22/12 She:] She saith: *P Pr.*
    22/14 Cometh the Dawn, and the Moth-Hour] Come the dawn with the
moth hour
    22/15 "Together with him, softly] softly, together *ts.*

FAMAM LIBROSQUE CANO (p. 22). *Reprinted: P Pr U P2.*
    22/23 then] *omitted P Pr U P2.*

THE CRY OF THE EYES (p. 24). *Reprinted: E U P2.*
    Title] The Eyes *E U P2.*

SCRIPTOR IGNOTUS (p. 24). *Reprinted: P.*
    Dedication] To K. R. H., *i.e. Katherine Ruth Heyman.*

DONZELLA BEATA (p. 26). *"Hilda's Book" (HB).*
    HB has prologue: Being alone where the way was full of dust, I said
"Era mea . . . Ad te coram veniam." And afterwards being come to a

woodland place where the sun was warm amid the autumn, my lips, striving to speak for my heart, formed those words which here follow.
Title] La Donzella Beata *HB*
27/1–2 this thing to bear / Again] again to bear / This thing *HB*
27/3 to] for *HB*
27/7 should] would *HB*
27/8–9 at the gate / Of high heaven, Star diadem'd] Star-diademmed at the gate / Of high heaven *HB*

Li Bel Chasteus (p. 28). *Reprinted: C. "Hilda's Book" (HB).*
HB adds a separate note, following another poem: Being before the vision of LI BEL CHASTEUS / "W'en as lang syne from shadowy castle towers / "Thy striving eyes did wander to discern / "Which compass point my homeward way should be."
28/6 torrent-wise] tumultuous *C.*
28/8 wandered] *omitted C.*
28/12 tide] time *C.*
28/13 But circle-arched, above the hum of life] But archèd high above the curl of life *C.*
28/15 runed] turned *C.*
28/19 While] When *C.*

Threnos (p. 30). *Reprinted: C P2.*
30/6 whirred the air] whirred in the air *C P2.*

Comraderie (p. 30). *Reprinted: C U P2. "Hilda's Book" (HB), and one ts. in the Pound Archive.*
Title] Era Venuta *HB.* Camaraderie *P Pr.*
Epigraph] *omitted HB.*
30/21 subtle] soft small *HB.*
31/1 bustling] dusty *HB ts.*
31/2 seemeth some-wise] seemth that some wise *ts.*
31/4 The air a while and giveth all things grace] My sight and shutteth out the world's disgrace *HB.* And shutteth out the world . . . and world's disgrace ⟨and all things base⟩ *ts.*
31/5–9 *HB omits, substitutes following:*
    That is apostacy of them that fail,
    Denying that God doth God's self disclose
    In every beauty that they will not see.
    Naethless when this sweetness comes to me
    I know thy thought doth pass as elfin "Hail"
    That beareth thee, as doth the wind a rose.
The ts. gives the above as an alternate third stanza, substituting only good doth gods *for* God doth God's *in the second line.*

Malrin (p. 33).
33/11 "Peace! hasten] "Peace!! (that is Silence!!) hasten *ts.*
Ts. has note: To give concrete for a symbol, to explain a parable, is

295

for me always a limiting, a restricting; yet, because some to whom this has already come have not seen into it, I will say this: that it arises from a perception how the all-soul of mankind is one and joineth itself wholly at some time and returneth to God as a bride. And he the great hero of the new things spiritual is whoso waiteth for all the rest aiding as he may, yet daring to be last.

Ezra Pound, Milligan Place,
Crawfordsville, Ind.

MASKS (p. 34). *Reprinted: P.*
34/13 Ere *etc.*] Ere Arthur kingly reigned at Camelot

ON HIS OWN FACE IN A GLASS (p. 34). *Reprinted: E U P2.*

THE TREE (p. 35). *Reprinted: C U P2.*
35/8 Knowing *etc.*] & Knew the truth of many hidden things *C(proofs).*
35/17 many new things] many a new thing *C U P2.*
35/18 were] was *C U P2.*
The Canzoni page proofs include notes to this poem; Pound considered extensive revision. In addition to the correction written in above at line 35/8 (not included in any published text) the following lines, appearing only in the proofs, are written in beneath line 35/10:
    Felt Daphne turn into a laurel tree
    & knew how Baucis & Philema could
    Be intertwined in memorial boughs
    after, the gods had been within their house.
The following lines are written in after line 35/18:
    Yes, I have stood with the secrecy
    Been where our wits gain mastery

PLOTINUS (p. 36). *Reprinted: E.*
Title] Plotinus, or The Cause *ts.*
Ts. has notes:
36/13 cone] The "cone" is I presume the "Vritta" whirl-pool, vortex-ring of the Yogi's cosmogony.
Footnote] Plotinus teaching "that one could not dwell alone but must ever bring forth souls from himself." The sonnet tho an accurate record of sensation and no mere (not) theorizing is in closer accord with a certain Hindoo teacher whose name I have not yet found.

PROMETHEUS (p. 37).
Title] *subtitled* How prometheus bore the flame in a hollow reed *ts.*

AEGUPTON (p. 37). *Reprinted: C P2.*
Title] De Aegypto *C P2.*
38/8 that] who *C P2.*
38/9 For] *omitted C P2.*

38/10 kiss] lips *C P2*.
38/15 unto] to *C*.
38/15–18] *omitted P2*.

BALLAD FOR GLOOM (p. 38). *Reprinted: P Pr The New Poetry (1917).*
Title] In tenebris cantum est *ts*.

FOR E[UGENE]. McC[ARTNEY]. (p. 39). *Reprinted: P Pr U P2. See also "The Rejected Stanza" in the San Trovaso Notebook, p. 250.*

SALVE O PONTIFEX! (p. 40). *Reprinted: R Poetry Review (Feb. 1912) L2. Except for negligible differences in spacing, the later versions published in R, Poetry Review, and L2 are identical. All include the following revisions of A.*
Title] Salve Pontifex (A. C. S.)
40/21 do] *omitted*.
40/23 Toning thy melodies even as winds tone] Intoning thy melodies as winds intone
40/24 The whisper *etc.*] The whisperings of leaves on sunlit days.
40/25 Even as] And
41/26 being Life's] that is life's
41/27–28] *omitted*.
41/29 And night] And of night
41/36 makest wine of song of] makest a wing of song
41/39 and the worship of love] *omitted*.
42/1 Wherefor tho] Though
42/1 co-novices bent] co-novices are bent
42/10 beauteous paons] paeans
42/12 of years] of thy years
42/13–14 music that men may not / Over readily understand] music
42/16 that evening] that the evening
42/28 Being] At being
42/29 mad'st canticles] madest thy canticles
R has note: This apostrophe was written three years before Swinburne's death. *L2 has same note with addition:* Balderdash but let it stay for the rhythm. E. P.

TO THE DAWN: DEFIANCE (p. 43). *Reprinted: E.*
Title] Defiance *E*.
43/28 can] shall *ts*.

THE DECADENCE (p. 44).
44/12 vivant] vivent *A corrected by editor*.

SONG (p. 46). *Reprinted: E Pr.*
46/6 'tis in] in my *ts*.

Motif (p. 46). *Reprinted: P.*
Title] Search *P*.

La Regina Avrillouse (p. 46). *Reprinted: Philadelphia Ledger (19 Mar. 1910).*

A Rouse (p. 47).
48/22 you] ye *ts*.
48/28 "jolif bachillier"!] merry gentlemen *ts*.

In Tempore Senectutis: An Anti-stave (p. 50).
Title] In tempore senectus *A*. *Corrected as above by editor.*

Prelude. Over the Ognisanti (p. 59). *ms(STN)*.
59/12 shades of song] songs *ms*.
59/13 Within] in *ms*.

Night Litany (p. 60). *Reprinted: E Pr U P2. ms(STN)*.
Title] Venetian Night Litany *ms*.
Ms. has note: No man having looked upon the ineffable things has any right to tarnish his portrayal thereof, with claims of ownership. Venice, May (?) June? *1908*.

Purveyors General (p. 61). *ms(STN)*.

Aube of the West Dawn (p. 63). *The Pound Archive has one typescript and one manuscript (STN).*
63/1 svelte] I *ts*.
63/2 robes] robe *ts*.
63/3 I] so *ts*.

To La Contessa Bianzafior (p. 63). *ms(STN)*.
Title] Difesa *ms(STN) with epigraph:* "And having given that which he had, went forth again." Gibel-Taraj March *1908*.
64/8] *Following this line ms. adds:* ("Eccovi gli anime mil avoi si Tornon!")

Partenza di Venezia (p. 65). *ms(STN)*.

Lucifer Caditurus (p. 66).
66/21 toward sympathy] co-sympathy *ms(STN)*.
67/10 *Following this line, ms. has five pages of fragmentary, canceled draft, in a very rough state, ending with the words:* God is a circle inescapable likewise his law.

Sandalphon (p. 67). *Reprinted: E.*

GREEK EPIGRAM (p. 70). *Reprinted: E Pr U. ms(STN).*
Title] Prayer *U.*
Ms(STN) adds footnote in Greek script: Ezra Pound ton poetei *with the date* 7. 29

CHRISTOPHORI COLUMBI TUMULUS (p. 71). *Reprinted: E. ms(STN).*
Ts. has notes:
Canceled] Written before America was known not to be India.
Footnote] The text of above is to be found in the "Ghero" collection, for notes on which see the author's articles in *Book News Monthly. The "Ghero" collection is a two-volume anthology of late Latin poetry, collected by Ranutius Gherus (pseudonym for Janus Gruterus), published at Frankfurt in 1608. Pound had published an article on the collection in Book News Monthly for February 1908. The Capilupus poem ("Epitaph. Christophori Columbi") on which Pound's translation is based occurs at page 644, Vol. I of the Ghero collection.*
Pound had sent the poem to Viola S. Baxter [Jordan] for possible magazine publication: Dear Viola. You may copy this (please) and try it on the "swells." Century, Harpers, Scribners. I didn't translate it here [*Venice*] as the typing shows, but Venice sounds more literatesque than C[*rawfords*]ville, [*Ind.*]
Harper's returned the submission to Baxter with the note: Dear Sir: We are returning herewith Mr. Ezra Pound's translation of "Christophori Columbi," as we never publish translations in our magazine.

HISTRION (p. 71). *First published: Evening Standard and St. James's Gazette, Lon. (26 Oct. 1908). Reprinted: E Current Literature (Mar. 1910) Pr.*
Ts. has footnote: "I do not teach—I awake" Ezra Pound

NEL BIANCHEGGIAR (p. 72). *First published: Evening Standard and St. James's Gazette, Lon. (8 Dec. 1908). Reprinted: E Italian version by Marco Londonio included at the back of P. ms(STN), dated: 7–29.*
Title] For Katherine Ruth Heyman. (After One of Her Venetian Concerts.) *Evening Standard.*

Contents of Personae (1909)
Grace before Song *—La Fraisne *—Cino *—Na Audiart *—Villonaud for this Yule *—A Villonaud: Ballad of the Gibbet *—Mesmerism *— Fifine Answers *—In tempore senectutis *—Famam librosque cano *— Scriptor ignotus *—Praise of Ysolt [incorporates "Vana"]—Camaraderie * —Masks *—Tally-O—Ballad for Gloom *—For E. Mc C.*—At the Heart o' Me—Xenia—Occidit—Search * [formerly "Motif"]—An Idyl for Glaucus—In Durance—Guillaume de Lorris Belated—In the Old Age of the Soul—Alba Belingalis—From Syria—From the Saddle—Marvoil—Re- volt, Against the Crepuscular Spirit in Modern Poetry—And Thus in

Nineveh—The White Stag—Piccadilly—Notes [*to the poems, including Marco Londonio's Italian version of "Nel Biancheggiar"*]
* Indicates poems reprinted from *A*.

PRAISE OF YSOLT (p. 79). *Reprinted: Pr U P2. See also "Vana," p. 27.*

AT THE HEART O' ME (p. 81). *Reprinted: Pr U.*

XENIA (p. 82). *See also "Lotus-bloom" (240/14–21), in STN.*

OCCIDIT (p. 82). *The poem was extensively revised in manuscript (STN), including the following variants:*
Title] Golden Sunset *with subtitle* from Opening of Scene in an Heroical play
82/21 *Ms. adds before this line:* Sing I the Spleandor[*sic*] to the measures old / Seek ye who will what tricks the time doth bear / I sing the Hour of Gold / Praise! If my speech be fair
82/21 breaks] ⟨gleams⟩ ⟨glows⟩ ⟨leaps⟩
82/22 on] ⟨of⟩
82/23 Neath] ⟨to⟩
82/25 Bear] ⟨Hold⟩
83/3 *Ms. follows with alternative line:* When kings there be to greet with honoring
83/4 Are hung king-greeting from the ponticells] ⟨From frail oer hanging ponticels drop low⟩
83/4 the] frail
83/5 And drag] dragging
83/6 figures live again] ⟨heros are reborn⟩
83/7 Wind-molden] ⟨Wind-shaken⟩ ⟨Wind-molded⟩
83/7 unto their life's erst guise] ⟨again [?] guise of life⟩ ⟨again unto lifes guise⟩
83/8 breath] breast
83/9 That] ⟨Where⟩
83/9 doth take] ⟨doth choose⟩ ⟨elects⟩
83/9 to house his soul] ⟨his soul to house⟩

AN IDYL FOR GLAUCUS (p. 83). *Reprinted: Pr.*
83/13 is] was *Pr.*
85/18 Have I] I have *Pr.*
The poem was extensively revised from typescript, including the following variants:
84/2 we it deem] we consider it
84/3 E'en] And
84/4 with me] to me
84/11 chide] blame
84/12 not my] me no

84/13 They mock me at the route, well, I have come again.] They mock me at their games. I come again.

84/14 Last night I saw three white forms move] And last night here I saw the three forms move

84/15 the white foam crest] the crest

84/16 I somehow knew] And knew somehow

84/21 E'en as he might after a long night's taking on the deep] Just as he might after a fishing-night

84/22 And when he woke . . . near to me] And woke with lips that were as kind to me

84/28 for the sea its charm] for this new sea-charm

84/29 leapt him in the wave] leapt into the wave

84/30 the] his

84/31 I know not any more how long it is] I do not know how long it is that I

84/32 Since I have dwelt not in my mother's house] Have lived thus wildly from my mother's house

85/1 the herb he offered unto me] the grass that he would have me eat

85/3 More wide-spanned power than old wives draw from them] A power more deep than old wives get from them

85/4 found I this grass] if I should find the grass

85/7 the two-foot coursers] two-footed coursers

85/8 fishers'] fishing

85/16 the wind doth seem] the wind seems now

85/17 To mock me now, all night, all night, and] To hold me mocked! All night, all night

85/18 Have I strayed among the cliffs here] I strayed among the cliffs. And they?

85/19 They say, some day I'll fall] They say I'll fall some day

85/23 within] between

85/27 I am quite tired now] And I am tired now

85/29 some little while] *omitted*

IN DURANCE (p. 86). *Reprinted: L2 U P2.*
86/14 yea] And *U P2.*
87/6–7] *omitted L2 U P2.*

IN THE OLD AGE OF THE SOUL (p. 91). *Reprinted: Pr.*

ALBA BELINGALIS (p. 91). *First published: Hamilton Literary Magazine (1905).*
Title] Belangal Alba *HLM*
91/15 splendour] glory *HLM*
91/19–20 *Refrain*] Dawn light, oer sea & hight, riseth bright
                    Passeth vigil, clear looketh on the night. *ms.*
91/20–21 *HLM omits, substitutes following:*

Dawn light, o'er sea and height, riseth bright
Passeth vigil, clear shineth on the night.
91/22 Whom the ambush] Whom ambush *ms.*
91/25–26 *Refrain*] Oer cliff & ocean white doth dawn appeareth
            Passeth vigil & the shadows cleareth *ms.*
91/26 It passeth] Passeth *HLM*
92/2 The stars] Stars *HLM*
92/5 is the dawn] is dawn *HLM ms.*

FROM SYRIA (p. 92).
The poem is extensively revised from manuscript, including the following variants.
subtitle] that he sent unto his lady in Provence, he being then in Syria, a crusader
92/10 Eke] And
92/10 singing] chanting
92/11 When] The
92/12 Then 'tis] 'Tis then
92/13 Do make mine] Maketh my
92/18 Be] Is
92/20 Wherefore should his fight the more be bold] & therefor should he fight more bold
92/21 Song bear I] Song I bear
92/22 Sith ire] For wrath
92/23 think I] I think
92/24 ne'er have I] have I ne'er
93/2 I will not] will I nowise
93/3 That sometime I'll have cause to sing] That somewhile I have cause ⟨place⟩ to sing
93/5 somewhile I'll] I somewhile
93/8 if e'er I come] if I come
93/16 Pardi, hath the wide world in fee] *Beneath this line in the ms. is the alternative version,* "Hath, as he knows, the world in fee" *with the notation:* "more literal but I don't like it"
93/21 that] the
93/23 and what of me to-morrow] what do I tomorrow

FROM THE SADDLE (p. 94).
Title] *A Diane* from the French of D'Aubigné *ms.*
94/1 wind and wave] wave & wind *ms.*
94/3 Behind me bay] Behind doth bay *ms.*
94/4 As hounds the tempests of my foes] As hound, a tempest cloud of foes *ms.*
94/6 Pistols my pillow's service pay] *Three alternative lines were considered in ms.:*
My arms beneath my head I lay
Pistols 'neath my head I lay
Asleep arms 'neath my head I lay

MARVOIL (p. 94). *Reprinted: Pr U P2.*

REVOLT. AGAINST THE CREPUSCULAR SPIRIT IN MODERN POETRY (p. 96). *Reprinted: Pr.*
97/6 Great] High *Pr.*

AND THUS IN NINEVEH (p. 97). *Reprinted: Literary Digest (Nov. 1909) Pr U P2.*

THE WHITE STAG (p. 98). *Reprinted: Pr U P2.*

PICCADILLY (p. 98). *Reprinted: Book News Monthly (Aug. 1909) Pr The New Poetry (1917).*

Contents of Exultations (1909)
  Guido Invites You Thus—Night Litany *—Sandalphon *—Sestina: Alta-forte—Piere Vidal Old—Ballad of the Goodly Fere—Hymn III—Sestina for Ysolt—Portrait, from "La mere inconnue"—"Fair Helena" by Rack-ham—Laudantes—Aux belles de Londres—Francesca—Greek Epigram *—Christophori Columbi tumulus *—Plotinus **—On His Own Face in a Glass **—Histrion *—The Eyes ** [formerly "The Cry of the Eyes"]—Defiance ** [formerly "To the Dawn: Defiance"]—Song ("Love thou thy dream") **—Nel Biancheggiar *—Nils Lykke—A song of the Virgin Mother—Planh for the Young English King—Alba innominata—Planh.
  * Indicates poems reprinted from Q.
  ** Indicates poems reprinted from A.

GUIDO INVITES YOU THUS (p. 107). *Reprinted: U P2.*

SESTINA: ALTAFORTE (p. 108). *First published: English Review (June 1909). Reprinted: Pr U P2.*

PIERE VIDAL OLD (p. 109). *Reprinted: L2 U P2.*

BALLAD OF THE GOODLY FERE (p. 112). *First published: English Review (Oct. 1909). Reprinted: Literary Digest (Oct. 1909) E Current Literature (Mar. 1910) Pr The New Poetry (1917) U P2.*

PORTRAIT (p. 115). *First published: English Review (Oct. 1909).*
Title] Un retrato [*sic*] *ER.*

"FAIR HELENA" BY RACKHAM (p. 116). *Reprinted: Pr.*

LAUDANTES DECEM PULCHRITUDINIS JOHANNAE TEMPLI (p. 117). *Reprinted: Pr U.*
Title] Laudantes *Pr.*
117/2 poor] uncertain *U.*

117/3 poor] *omitted U.*
117/4 the wistful throng] those *U.*
117/5 That hopeless] Who *U.*
117/23 *note:* the Beloved] her *U.*

AUX BELLES DE LONDRES (p. 120). *Reprinted: U.*

FRANCESCA (p. 121). *Reprinted: U P2.*

NILS LYKKE (p. 121). *First published: English Review (Oct. 1909). Reprinted: Pr U. The U version is extensively revised. The first stanza reads as follows:*
　　Infinite memories.
　　Why are you forever calling and murmuring in the dark there?
　　And reaching out your hands
　　　　　between me and my beloved?
121/20 will you be ever a-casting] are you forever casting *U.*
121/23 a-glinting] glinting *U.*

A SONG OF THE VIRGIN MOTHER (p. 122). *Reprinted: Pr.*
Pr adds concluding stanza:
　　Ya veis que no tengo
　　Con que guardarlo,
　　O angeles santos
　　Que vais volando
　　Por que duerme mi niño
　　Tened los ramos!

PLANH FOR THE YOUNG ENGLISH KING (p. 123). *Reprinted: Pr U P2.*

ALBA INNOMINATA (p. 125). *Reprinted: Pr U.*

PLANH (p. 126). *Reprinted: Pr U.*
Title] Of White Thoughts he saw in a Forest *U.*
U version, otherwise identical, has this first stanza:
　　Heavy with dreams,
　　Thou who art wiser than love,
　　Though I am hungry for their lips
　　　　When I see them a-hiding
　　And a-passing out and in through the shadows
　　　　In the pine wood,
　　And they are white, like the clouds in the sky's forest
　　Ere the stars arise to their hunting;

Canzoni. The thirteen selections from C which were first published in Pr were gathered together under the heading: Canzoniere / Studies in Form

CANZON. THE YEARLY SLAIN (p. 133). *First published: English Review (Jan. 1910). Reprinted: Pr (with Frederic Manning's "Kore") C Selected Poems (1928).*

Footnote to ts: "Kore" or Maiden is especially used of Persephone with regard to her being stolen by Lord of Dis—and thereby causing death of summer.

Ts. note, sent to Pound's parents, accompanying copies of the three "Canzoni" which appeared in the English Review in Jan. 1910 ("The Yearly Slain"; "Canzon: To Be Sung Beneath a Window"; and "Canzon: The Spear"): I send mss. of Canzoni to appear in The Eng. *Rev.* Chief charm being that they say nothing *in* particular. They are made simply for their music. 1st one to speak the 2nd and 3rd to be sung. The complicated "rhyme" is to be noted. E. P.

Canceled note at back of C(proofs): The canzoni have already been assailed and on this account [I] feel that I may be permitted to venture toward that dangerous thing, an explanation; or rather, I ask you to consider whether it be not more difficult to serve that love of Beauty (or, even of some particular sort of Beauty) which belongs to the permanent part of oneself, than to express some sudden emotion or perception which being unusual, being keener than normal, is by its very way being, clearly defined or at least set apart from those things of the mind among which it appears.

The canzone is to me rather a ritual, the high mass, if you will, of poetry, than its prayer in secret.

The forms I have used are in their order those of Arnaut Daniel; Sols sui que sai (with a slight error) of Rudel; Song to the Lady of Tripoli.

Amor di lonh.

Piere Vidal's, Ab l'alen tir vas me l'aire.

Daniel's Doutz brais e critz.

Dante's, Voi che intendendo il terzo ciel movete.

Daniel's, Sols sui que sai lo sobrafan quem sortz (correctly).

The rhythms in the second and third canzoni are, as any should perceive, for singing and not for speaking.

CANZON. THE SPEAR (p. 134). *First published: English Review (Jan. 1910). Reprinted: Pr C. The Pound Archive has two mss. and one ts.*

Pr adds note: This fashion of stanza is used by Jaufre Rudel in the song "D'un amor de lonh." The measure is to be sung rather than spoken.

134/20 clear light] clear far light *ms. 1 ER.*

136/1 My love is lovelier] That one who is lovelier *ms. 1 ts.*

Ms. 2 is a fragment; stanza I was abandoned in the published text, II and III correspond, with extensive variants, to I and II in the published text:

I

When April's green the land arrays
And her breath freeth prisoned waters,
Tis meet that men should make good lays
Where words run free as April waters.
When ferns their conquering banners spread,
When crocus putteth off his dread
My song shall no more hide, afraid ⟨delayed⟩

II

'Tis the clear light of love I praise
That glanceth o'er life's sombre waters.
A clarity that gleams always
Though man's soul pass through troubled waters
Strange ways to him are openèd
To shore the beaten bark is led
If only love of light give aid.

III

Ah for that far gold spear-point's blaze
Whose shaft is lain upon the waters
Ah might I pass upon those rays
To where she gleams o'er the waters
or might my troubled heart be fed
Upon the frail clear light there shed
Then were my pain at last allayed.

CANZON. TO BE SUNG BENEATH A WINDOW (p. 139). *First published: English Review (Jan. 1910). Reprinted: Pr C.*
Ms. note, C(proofs): plucked strings
136/21 by] with *ts.*
137/12 that] which *ts. ER.*
137/15 praise] song *ts. ER.*
Pr adds note: The form and measure are those of Piere Vidal's "Ab l'alen tir vas me l'aire." The song is fit only to be sung, and is not to be spoken.

CANZON. OF INCENSE (p. 137). *First published: English Review (Apr. 1910). Reprinted: Pr C Selected Poems (1928).*
Pr adds note: To this form sings Arnaut Daniel, with seven stanzas instead of five.

CANZONE. OF ANGELS (p. 139). *First published: Pr. Reprinted: Fortnightly Review (Feb. 1912).*
Pr adds note: This form is not Provençal, but that of Dante's matchless "Voi che intendendo il terzo ciel movete." *Il Convito,* II, bar the deca-

syllabic lines which one can scarcely escape in English but which do not, despite all statements to the contrary, correspond to the hendecasyllabic lines in the Italian.

To Our Lady of Vicarious Atonement (p. 141). *First published: Pr.*

To Guido Cavalcanti (p. 142). *First published: Pr.*
Title] Epilogue: To Guido Cavalcanti *Pr.*
142/8 Ser Guido of Florence] O Messire Guido *Pr.*
Pr adds note: This poem foreruns a translation of "The Sonnets and Ballate of Guido" now in preparation.

Sonnet in Tenzone (p. 142). *First published: Pr.*

Sonnet. Chi è Questa? (p. 143). *First published: Pr.*

Ballata, Fragment (p. 143). *First published: Pr.*
Ms. note, C(proofs): canta voce
Title] Of Grace *Pr.*

Canzon. The Vision (p. 144). *First published: Forum, NY (Oct. 1910).*
Reprinted: Pr C.
Ms. note, C(proofs): bowed strings and muted cello
Title] "Ivory to gold o heart o heart" *ms.*
145/30 Thou royal-souled] Ah, Royal-souled *Forum.*
Pr adds note: The form is that of Arnaut Daniel's "Sols sui que sai lo sobrafan quem sortz."

Octave (p. 146). *First published: Pr.*

Sonnet. The Tally Board (p. 146). *First published: Pr.*
146/16 bought] brought *Pr.*

Ballatetta (p. 147). *Reprinted: P2.*

Era Mea (p. 148). *First published: The Book of the Poets' Club (1909).*
See also, Latin epigraph to "Donzella Beata," p. 26, and note. (C follows "Era Mea" with "Threnos" and "The Tree," reprinted from A.)

Paracelsus in Excelsis (p. 148). *First published: The Book of the Poets' Club (1909). Reprinted: Pr (in E section although not originally published in E) C P2. (C follows this poem with "De Aegypto" [formerly "Aegupton"] and "Li Bel Chasteus," reprinted from A.)*

Prayer for His Lady's Life (p. 149). *Reprinted: L2 P2.*

SPEECH FOR PSYCHE (p. 149). *Reprinted: P2.*
  149/15 and as] as *ms.*
  149/15 among] amid *ms.*
  149/18 petals of flowers] petal of flower *ms.*
  149/19 Waver] waves *ms.*
  149/19 seem] seems *ms.*
  149/21 And closer me] yet closer to me *ms.*
  149/24] *Ms. omits, adds following:*
    the waves are not more
    gentle when we dive
    through them or glide upon their
    backs and he, the night,
    the power to [?], lay there
    like breath
      light light upon the water

"BLANDULA, TENULLA, VAGULA" (p. 150). *Reprinted: L2 P2.*

ERAT HORA (p. 150). *Reprinted: L2 P2.*

EPIGRAMS. I, II (p. 151). *First published: The Book of the Poets' Club
(1909) [I only]. Reprinted: L2 [II only].*

THE GOLDEN SESTINA (p. 152).
  153/1 When, then, I] And when I *C(proofs).*
  153/6 her delicate fair face] fair and delicate her face *C(proofs).*
  Note, canceled in C(proofs): I must say in justice to certain other poems
  in this volume that I did not find Pico's sestina until after I had
  written them.

ROME (p. 154). *Reprinted: L2 P2.*
  Ms. note, C(proofs): spoken quality in organum
  154/3 worn] grown *ms.*
  154/4 within these walls keeps] in these grey wall hath *ms.*
  154/8 She is Time's prey] Time's prey she is *ms.*
  154/11 transient and seaward bent] that runs toward the sea *ms.*
  154/12 Rome. O world, thou unconstant mime] ah world's inconstancy
  ⟨incontinent⟩ *ms.*
  154/13 in thee Time batters] lo time doth batter *ms.*
  154/14 And] But *C(proofs).*
  154/14 And that which fleeteth doth outrun swift time] Gainst that
  which fleeteth is swift time [?] *ms.*

HER MONUMENT, THE IMAGE CUT THEREON (p. 155). *Reprinted: P2.*
  Title] Upon the image of her monument *ms.*
  155/1–3] O glance, whose very present steadfastness / had made men
  tremble, / & o lip turned high *ms.*

VICTORIAN ECLOGUES (p. 156). *Reprinted: P2 [II only, "Satiemus"].*
158/7 Oh] And
158/16 gave me answer and] keened mine answer *C(proofs).*
158/18 chill] still *C(proofs).*
158/23 Will I once] Yet will I *C(proofs).*
158/28 And] Still *C(proofs).*
C(proofs) adds the canceled lines, concluding III, "Abelard":
    Wherefore, O father of all wandered souls,
    Grant me to-night my boon and let the wings
    Of my protection keep all trouble out
    From her dear breast.
Aude caelicolo!

A PROLOGUE (p. 159). *First published: Sunday School Times, Phila. (Dec. 3, 1910) as "Christmas Prologue."*

MAESTRO DI TOCAR (p. 162). *W.R. is Walter Morse Rummel.*

L'ART (p. 163).
163/2 are shown] seem but *C(proofs).*

SONG IN THE MANNER OF HOUSMAN (p. 163). *Reprinted: L2 P2.*
Title] Housman's Message to Mankind *L2.* Mr. Housman's Message *P2.*

TRANSLATIONS FROM HEINE (p. 164). *Reprinted: L2 P2.*
165/13 When light their voices lift them up] So soft their voices, lifted up *ms.*
165/14 against the ear] upon the air *ms.*
165/15 Through trills and runs like crystal] run and run and run, crystal *ms.*
C(proofs) has ms. addition at back of volume:
    I bless the sun & moon
    & stars of heaven.
    I bless the little birds
    that sing at even.
    I bless the sea & land
    & the flowers of the common.
    I bless the violets that are soft
    as the eyes of my woman
    your violet eyes beloved,
    & I love life thru' thee!
    Hallowed the Tree be
    Where Thou gavest thyself to me.
Heine.

Pound Archive has ms. fragment:
    Seldom have I understood you,

& you give me poor attention.
Tis only when we meet ⟨sleep⟩ in bed
We get more facile comprehension.

UND DRANG (p. 167). *Reprinted: L2 U[XII] P2[VII–XII].*
171/18 virtues] powers *ms.*
171/19 the four-square walls of standing time] the walls of time that
stand four-square *ms.*
171/29 Say] Are *ms.*
171/30 That man doth pass the net] A man goes out beyond *C(proofs).*
171/30 That] How *ms.*
171/31 time is shrivelled] all time shrivels *ms.*
172/2–3 *omitted P2.*
172/15 Sapphire Benacus *etc.*] God set his sign in colour of Lake Garda
ms.
172/16–17 *Lines reversed in order ms.*
172/16 herself's turned] herself turns *ms.*
172/18–20 *omitted ms.*
172/24 Who] That *ms.*
Ms. has footnote to "Au Jardin": This page will naturally be compre-
hended by none but true lovers.

SILET (p. 181). *First published: Smart Set (May 1912). Reprinted: L2
U P2.*
Title] omitted L2.
U and P2 add note: Verona, 1911.

IN EXITUM CUIUSDAM (p. 182). *Reprinted: L2 U P2.*

APPARUIT (p. 182). *First published: English Review (May 1912). Reprinted:
L2 U P2.*

THE TOMB AT AKR ÇAAR (p. 183). *Reprinted: L2 U P2.*

PORTRAIT D'UNE FEMME (p. 184). *Reprinted: Smart Set (Nov. 1913) L2 U
P2.*

N[EW]. Y[ORK]. (p. 185). *Reprinted: Smart Set (Sept. 1913) The New
Poetry (1917) L2 U P2.*
U adds note: Madison Ave. 1910

A GIRL (p. 186). *Reprinted: Smart Set (Sept. 1913) L2 U P2.*

"PHASELLUS ILLE" (p. 186). *Reprinted: Smart Set (Oct. 1913) L2 U P2.*

AN OBJECT (p. 187). *Reprinted: L2 U P2.*

Quies (p. 187). *Reprinted: L2 U P2.*

The Seafarer (p. 188). *First published: The New Age (November, 1911). Reprinted: Cathay (1915) U P2.*
New Age adds: Philological note.—The text of this poem is rather confused. I have rejected half of line 76 ["Daring ado, . . ." *(190/3)—ed.*], read "Angles" for angels in line 78, and stopped translating before the passage about the soul and the longer lines beginning, "Mickle is the fear of the Almighty," and ending in a dignified but platitudinous address to the Deity: "World's elder, eminent creator, in all ages, amen." There are many conjectures as to how the text came into its present form. It seems most [most *canceled by hand in Pound's copy*] likely that a fragment of the original poem, clear through about the first thirty lines, and thereafter increasingly illegible, fell into the hands of a monk with literary ambitions, who filled in the gaps with his own guesses and "improvements." The groundwork may have been a longer narrative poem, but the "lyric," as I have accepted it, divides fairly well into "The Trials of the Sea," its Lure, and the Lament for Age.

Echoes (p. 191). *First published: North American Review (Jan. 1912).*
subtitle] NAR adds: (Trecento)
191/6–11 *omitted NAR.*
191/12 Till] For *NAR.*
191/26 This] So *NAR.*

An Immorality (p. 192). *First published: Poetry Review (Feb. 1912) with "For a beery voice" and "After Heine," under the heading "Oboes." Reprinted: Smart Set (Sept. 1913).*

Dieu! Qu'il la Fait (p. 192). *First published: Poetry Review (Feb. 1912). Reprinted: L2 U P2. (C follows this poem with "Salve Pontifex," reprinted from A.)*

Δώρια [Doria] (p. 193). *First published: Poetry Review (Feb. 1912). Reprinted: Des Imagistes (1914) The New Poetry (1917) L2 U P2.*

The Needle (p. 193). *Reprinted: L2 U P2.*

Sub Mare (p. 194). *First published: Poetry Review (Feb. 1912). Reprinted: Smart Set (Sept. 1913) L2 U P2.*

Plunge (p. 194). *Reprinted: L2 U P2.*
194/24 Oh, but far out] Oh, to be out *L2.*

A Virginal (p. 195). *Reprinted: Smart Set (Sept. 1913) L2 U P2.*
195/3 has] hath *U P2.*

PAN IS DEAD (p. 196). *Reprinted: Smart Set (Sept. 1913) L2 U P2. Note: punctuated as dialogue U P2.*

THE PICTURE (p. 197). *Reprinted: L2 U P2.*

OF JACOPO DEL SELLAIO (p. 197). *Reprinted: L2 P2.*

THE RETURN (p. 198). *First published: English Review (June 1912). Reprinted: Des Imagistes (1914) The New Poetry (1917) L2 U P2.*

EFFECTS OF MUSIC (p. 199). *Reprinted: U.*

EZRA ON THE STRIKE (p. 203). *Reprinted: Poetry Australia, No. 46, 1973, with the following comment:* . . . it is based upon the coal strike of 1902, which, as it progressed from November into December, left Philadelphia seriously short of coal for heating, so that some families closed their houses and went to apartment buildings or hotels. The Philadelphia newspapers reported "much distress among the poor". . . .
Although most of the evidence suggests that this is Pound's composition, one small doubt remains. William Barnes Lower published a number of similar poems, both signed and unsigned, in the *Times-Chronicle,* about the same time, and it is just possible that "Ezra on the Strike" was from his pen. However, when some of his poems . . . were collected in 1954 . . . "Ezra on the Strike" was not among them. *(Carl Gatter and Noel Stock, "E.P.'s Pennsylvania")*

TO THE RAPHAELITE LATINISTS (p. 205).
"Weston Llewmys" was a pseudonym sometimes used by Ezra Pound in his early writings. See pp. 58, 69.

THERSITES: ON THE SURVIVING ZEUS (p. 206).
206/26] [of] *emended by editor from apparent error in published text.*

FOR A BEERY VOICE (p. 208). *Reprinted: U. In Poetry Review (Feb. 1912) this poem was published with "After Heine" and "An Immorality," under the heading "Oboes."*

EPILOGUE (p. 209). *This poem, first published in Collected Shorter Poems (1968), was submitted to Poetry magazine in 1912. The five books referred to are:* The Spirit of Romance, Canzoni, Ripostes, The Sonnets and Ballate of Guido Cavalcanti, The Canzoni of Arnaut Daniel.

Note to the poems withdrawn from *Canzoni*
Ezra Pound had originally intended to include in Canzoni *three additional sonnets, two additional longer poems, and some notes. This material was set up by the printers and is present in page proofs sent to*

the author between the 13th and 22nd of May, 1911. These proofs are now in the Humanities Research Center of the University of Texas, and we are grateful for the permission to reprint them here.

LEVIORA: I, II, IV (pp. 213–214). *These three sonnets, together with "L'Art" (numbered III in the proofs), formed a group with the title "Leviora". Only "L'Art" was included in the published volume (see p. 163).*

TO HULME (T. E.) AND [DESMOND] FITZGERALD (p. 214). *This poem follows "Leviora" in C(proofs). Published: Des Imagistes (1914) with note:* Written for the cenacle of 1909 vide Introduction to "The Complete Poetical Works of T. E. Hulme," published at end of *Ripostes.*

REDONDILLAS, OR SOMETHING OF THAT SORT (p. 215). *Published: Poetry Australia (Apr. 1967). This poem follows "To Hulme" and "Song in the Manner of Housman" in C(proofs).*
Title] Locksley hall, forty years further *C(proofs).*
221/34] *Second the canceled in C(proofs), but it seems to be necessary to the meter.*
Pound's notes, canceled in C(proofs): Fifty years ago one would have called this effusion "the Age."
      Note on the Proper Names in the Redondillas
Yeats (W. B.), specialist in renaissances.
T. Roosevelt (Theodore), president of one of the American republics early in the twentieth century. Not to be confused with Theodoric, Gothorum imperator.
Plarr, V. G., of the Rhymers' Club.
Vance, an American painter, chief works: "Christ appearing on the Waters" (Salon, Paris, '03) and the new bar-room in San Diego.
Whiteside, an American landscape painter.
Bergson, French postpragmatical philosopher.
Klimt of Vienna, and Zwintscher of Leipzig. Two too modern painters.
Spinoza, the particular passages I had in mind run as follows:
    "The more perfection a thing possesses the more it acts, and the less it suffers, and conversely the more it acts, the more perfect it is." *On the power of the intellect or human liberty. Proposition* xl.
    "When the mind contemplates itself and its power of acting, it rejoices, and it rejoices in proportion to the distinctness with which it imagines itself and its power of action." *Origin and Nature of the Affects,* xiii.
And another passage for which I cannot at the moment give the exact references, where he defines "The intellectual love" of anything as "The understanding of its perfections".

THE ALCHEMIST (p. 225). *Reprinted: P2. The text of "The Alchemist" was edited from five typescript pages, with manuscript corrections, and two manuscript pages with variants, now in the Pound Archive. The published text follows Umbra (1920); the poem was first published there with the note "Unpublished 1912."*

POEMS FROM THE SAN TROVASO NOTEBOOK

This section of the present edition completes the publication of the English poems from the San Trovaso Notebook, a small copybook of poems which Ezra Pound compiled while in Venice in 1908. Nine of these poems, plus two sections of another, were included in *A Quinzaine for this Yule* (1908); one more and a greatly reduced version of another (see note below to "Lotus-Bloom") appeared in *Personae* (1909). Two additional poems from the notebook were published by Vanni Scheiwiller in *A Lume Spento, 1908–1958* (Milan, 1958), and ten more poems, plus two sections of another, were selected by Mary de Rachewiltz for publication in *A Lume Spento and Other Early Poems* (New York, 1965). For the last volume Ezra Pound contributed a brief "Foreword" and Mary de Rachewiltz an important commentary, which we here reprint as an introduction to the poems from the notebook.

A collection of stale creampuffs. "Chocolate creams, who hath forgotten you?"

At a time when Bill W. was perceiving the "Coroner's Children."

As to why a reprint? No lessons to be learned save the depth of ignorance, or rather the superficiality of non-perception—neither eye nor ear. Ignorance that didn't know the meaning of "Wardour Street."

E.P.

San Ambrogio
19 Ag. '64

During the latter part of his stay in Venice in 1908, my father lived in the San Trovaso quarter of the city. The poems he wrote at that time are preserved in holograph in a small copybook of the kind which Italian schoolchildren still use for their exercises. It bears the legend "At San Trovaso" on the cover label. For the most part the poems appear to be fair copies of the final versions, though there are some pages of revisions and uncompleted drafts.

The importance of this period in his literary life may be guessed from the way he has woven it into the fabric of the *Cantos*. Briefly at first in Canto 3:

> I sat on the Dogana's steps
> For the gondolas cost too much that year.

But years later in the *Pisan Cantos* he gives more detail (Canto 76), including the time and place of the composition of these "San Trovaso" poems:

> well, my window
> looked out on the Squero where Ogni Santi
> meets San Trovaso
> things have ends and beginnings.

He was not entirely confident about his first book *A Lume Spento*, then in the process of being printed by A. Antonini at Venice:

> shd/I chuck the lot into the tide-water?
> le bozze "A Lume Spento"/
> and by the column of Todero
> shd/I shift to the other side.

Happily, he did not chuck the proofs into the canal, and went on writing poems that summer. The words "shift to the other side," apart from referring to his "contemplating a different way of life" (as he explained to me recently), may be taken to mean "crossing the Grand Canal." As the gondolas were expensive, he would walk over the Ponte dell'Accademia—referred to in the *Pisan Cantos* as "the new bridge of the Era"—and buy himself baked sweet potatoes at the corner cook-stall. His supper consisted mainly of a plate of *minestra d'orzo,* barley soup—"in my time/an orzo" (Canto 102).

What happened to the San Trovaso Notebook after his stay in Venice is difficult to follow. Some of the poems in it were published in the Christmas pamphlet *A Quinzaine for This Yule,* when he moved to London toward the end of 1908. After that, it seems to disappear until about ten years ago when I found it, in my grandfather's trunk, for Homer L. Pound was a conscientious collector of his son's papers. Not long afterward I asked my father's permission to publish some of the poems in it which seemed worth preserving. I received a very scathing answer. But his Italian publisher Vanni Scheiwiller persisted, and finally consent was given for "Statement of Being" and "For Italico Brass" to be included in the little volume dedicated to *A Lume Spento* which appeared in Scheiwiller's Pesce d'Oro series in commemoration of the fiftieth anniversary of Ezra Pound's first book and his seventy-third birthday.

Now the poet's attitude towards his earliest work is somewhat less severe, although his critical standards have not wavered—as can be judged from the foreword to this new edition. When recently I suggested that while this early work may not help "the young" technically, the feelings expressed in it might teach a lesson in this age of rage and cynicism, and that therefore it can be offered not merely as a "literary curiosity" but as further evidence of what stuff a young poet's dreams should be made of, he seemed satisfied.

Le Paradis n'est pas artificiel
States of mind are inexplicable to us

Brunnenburg, 1964   MARY DE RACHEWILTZ

The San Trovaso Notebook contains 78 leaves (156 pages), plus a paper wrapper. On the front label Pound has written "At San Trovaso," with the year "08" below. The date indicates the year of compilation, not necessarily of composition, for Pound has given earlier dates to some of the poems in the notebook. The materials were perhaps originally compiled with a view toward publishing a new collection of poems, as Pound seems to indicate by a table of contents written on the last page, and by a penciled "Envoi" written in the notebook after the last poem listed in the table ("For Italico Brass"). All the poems in the table are copied in ink: in black ink up through the second line of "For E. McC. The Rejected Stanza," and from there on in red ink, except for a few penciled passages. The collection did not originally begin with the first poem in the table ("Over the Ognisanti"), for the first leaf in the notebook has been evenly torn off about one inch from the margin, leaving the first word or two of 13 lines. This poem has not yet been identified. Additions and revisions were then made, with later materials clearly indicated by use of pencil, very dark ink, or a looser hand.

Pound's original practice was to use only the right-hand side of each leaf; but after the copying of the poems listed in the table had been completed, Pound here and there wrote additional materials on the blank left-hand pages; these consist of frequent revisions, an effort at an Italian translation of "Nel Biancheggiar," and two independent poems or poetical fragments. Such additional materials also appear in the spaces beneath the copied poems. After the "Envoi" Pound has used both sides of the leaf to compose in pencil a 6-page piece, with 3 pages canceled, bearing the title "Lucifer" (published in *Q:* see above, p. 66 and note, p. 298). The fifth and sixth leaves from the end contain, on the left-hand page, penciled jottings related to "Lucifer." On the second and third leaves from the end, two additional poems are copied in red ink, but these are written vertically on the left-hand pages, as though to distinguish them clearly from the other poems in the book; and rightly so, for these two ("Statement of Being" and "Das Babenzorn") are done in a comic mode out of tone with the rest of the book. Miscellaneous jottings of various kinds appear in the book in other places. On the inside of the front wrapper Pound has written the names of people who were apparently to receive complimentary copies of *Quinzaine,* and on the inside of the back wrapper he has written a similar list, apparently relating to *A Lume Spento.*

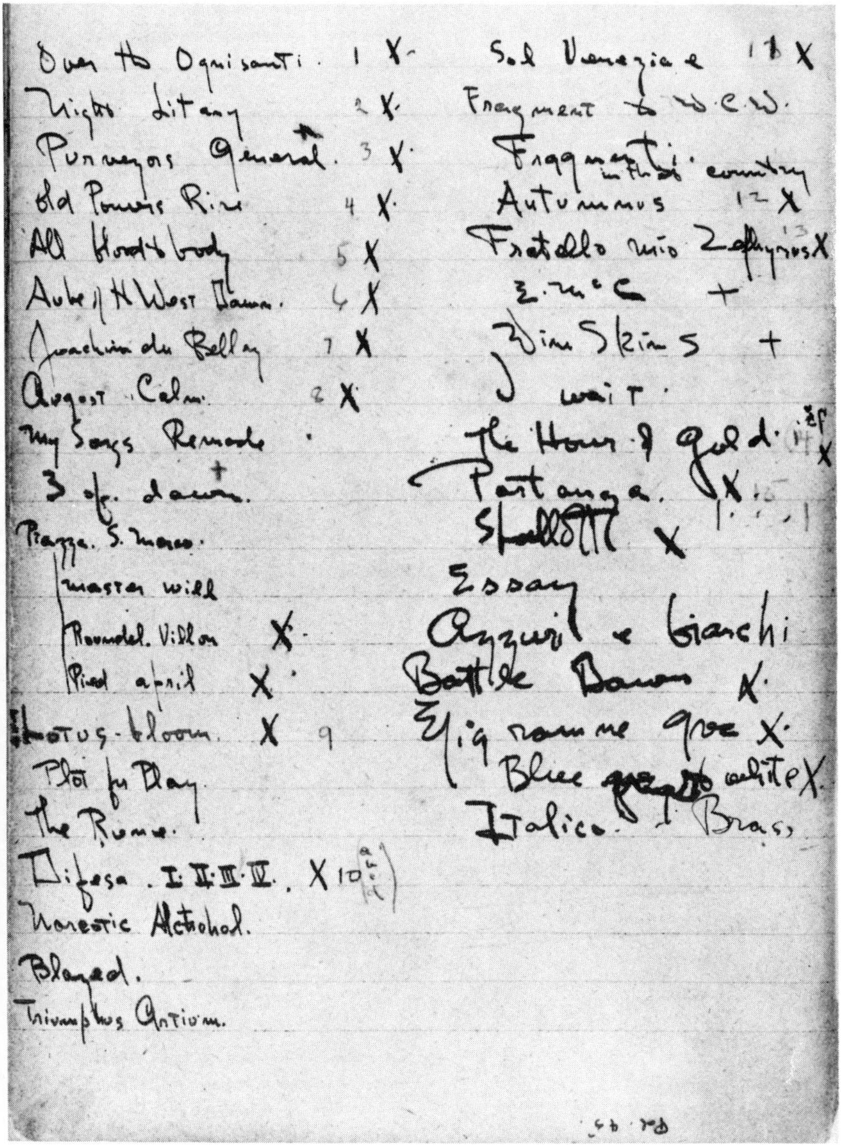
Over the Ognisanti 1 X
Night Litany 2 X
Purveyors General 3 X
Old Powers Rise 4 X
All [illegible] body 5 X
Aube of the West Dawn 6 X
Joachim du Bellay 7 X
August Calm 8 X
My Songs Remade
3 of dawn
Piazza S. Marco
master will
Roundel. Villon X
Pied april X
Lotus-bloom X 9
Plot for Play
The Rune
Difesa I. II. III. IV. X 10
Narcotic Alcohol
Blazed.
Triumphus [illegible]

Sol Veneziae 11 X
Fragment to W.C.W.
Fragmenti in that country
Autumnus 12 X
Fratello mio Zephyrus 13 X
E. McC +
Wine Skins +
I wait
The House of Gold 14 X
Partenza. X 15
Shalott X
Essay
Azzurri e bianchi
Battle Dawn X
Epigramme que X
Blue-grey & white X
Italia. Bras

Pound's table of contents in the San Trovaso Notebook

POUND'S TABLE OF CONTENTS IN THE SAN TROVASO NOTEBOOK

After the title or identifying phrase assigned to each poem in Pound's table, we have given, in parenthesis, the title as contained in the STN text, whenever this differs from the table. Previous publication of each poem is noted, together with variations in title in the early editions.

Over the Ognisanti. *Published in Q, with title* "Prelude. Over the Ognisanti": *see above, p. 59.*

Night Litany. ("Venetian Night Litany.") *Published in Q: see above, p. 60.*

Purveyors General. *Published in Q: see above, p. 61.*

Old Powers Rise ("San Vio. June": *see above, p. 233.) Published in A(1965).*

All blood and body. ("Roundel for Arms": *see above, p. 234.) Published in A(1965).*

Aube of the West Dawn. *Published in Q, with title* "Aube of the West Dawn. Venetian June": *see above, p. 63.*

Joachim du Bellay. ("Roundel. After Joachim du Bellay": *see above, p. 234.) Published in A(1965).*

August Calm. ("Sonnet of the August Calm": *see above, p. 235.) Published in A(1965).*

My Songs Remade. ("To Ysolt. For Pardon": *see above, p. 235.) Published in A(1965).*

3 of dawn. ("For Ysolt. The Triad of Dawn": *see above, p. 236.)*

Piazza S. Marco. ("Piazza San Marco. June": *see above, p. 238.)*

Master Will. *Published in A(1965).*

Roundel Villon. *Published in A(1965), first stanza only.*

Pied April. ("XCVIII.") *Published in A(1965).*

Lotus-bloom. *See above, p. 239.*

Plot for Play. ("For a play. (Maeterlinck)": *see above, p. 241.)*

The Rune. *See above, p. 242.*

Difesa. I. II. III. IV. *Parts I and II were published in Q, with the title* "To La Contessa Bianzafior (cent. xiv). (Defense at Parting)." *The bare numerals* "III" *and* "IV" *followed in Q, but these sections were not published until A(1965), when the two remaining sections were printed in their proper position; we have also printed the sections in this position: see above, p. 63.*

Narcotic Alchohol [*sic*]. *See above, p. 242.*

Blazed. *See above, p. 243.*

Triumphus Artium. ("For the Triumph of the Arts": *see above, p. 244.)*

Sol Veneziae. ("Alma Sol Veneziae. (Baritone)": *see above, p. 246.) Published in A(1965).*

Fragment to W. C. W. ("Fragment to W. C. W.'s Romance": *see above, p. 246.)*

["Christophori Columbi Tumulus" *follows here in the notebook, but is omitted from Pound's table. Published in Q: see above, p. 71.*]

Fragmenti. *See above, p. 248.*

Rondel. after. Joachim du Bellay.   10

I come unto thee thro' the hidden ways,
Soul of my soul, whose beauty quivereth
Within her eyes; to whom my former days,
As wined libation poured, while my breath
Strove to her homage in unskillful lays
Yet bade my heart make his high vaunt
                                    gainst death.

I come unto thee thro' the hidden ways
Who art the soul of beauty, & whose praise
On color, or light, or song championeth,
And of whom Time as but an herald saith.
'Trust (tho thou sense not, spite of my delays
Her whom I bring thee
                    thro' the hidden ways.

ref. J. d. B. (de celestial beauty)
& such as above to take her as promise
A greater thing:
    finding them in the beginning.
    position of those sounds
                    of la reflere.
                        in the works   J Tobit
                            deifyingg.

in that country. *This phrase, inserted as an afterthought at this point, occurs in the middle (249/3) of an untitled poem in the STN text: see above, p. 248.*

Autumnus. *See above, p. 249.*

Fratello mio Zephyrus. *See above, p. 250.*

E. McC. ("For E. McC. The Rejected Stanza": *see above, p. 250.*)

Wine Skins. ("Ballad of Wine Skins": *see above, p. 251.*) *Published in A(1965).*

I wait. *See above, p. 251.*

The Hour of Gold. *Published in P, with the title "Occidit": see above, p. 82.*

Partanza[*sic*]. *Published in Q, with the title "Partenza di Venezia": see above, p. 65.*

Shallott[*sic*]. *See above, p. 252.*

Essay. *See below, p. 322.*

Azzuri e bianchi. *Italian version of* "Blue grey and white"; *for the different version by Marco Londonio, see above, p. 100.*

Battle Dawn. *See above, p. 253.*

Epigramme Grec. *Published in Q, with the title "Greek Epigram": see above, p. 70.*

Blue grey and white. *Published in Q, with the title "Nel Biancheggiar": see above, p. 72. On a separate page following this poem Pound has written out a Biblical passage, II Chronicles.14.11.*

Italico Brass. ("For Italico Brass": *see above, p. 253.*) *Published in A(1958), incomplete.*

ROUNDEL. AFTER JOACHIM DU BELLAY (p. 234).

 STN has note: ref. J.d.B (to the celestial beauty) such as chose to take them as promise of a greater thing, finding them in the position of that sonnet beginning, *oltre la sphere,* in the works of the great [– – – – ?], I forbid art so to do.

SONNET OF THE AUGUST CALM (p. 235). *HB.*

 Title] "To draw back into the soul of things." PAX *HB.*

 235/1 When Summer hath her noon, it likes me lie] Meseemeth that tis sweet this wise to lie *HB.*

 235/5 weirds of dream] thoughts of thee *HB.*

 235/5 glide] ⟨float⟩ *STN.*

 235/8 runes] ⟨things⟩ *HB.*

 235/9 sooth] ⟨things⟩ ⟨truth⟩ *STN.*

 235/9–14 *HB omits, substitutes:*

  Such peace as this would make deaths self most sweet
  Could I but know, Thou maiden of the sun.
  That thus thy presence would go forth with me
  Unto that shadow land where ages feet
  Have wandered, and where life's dreaming done,
  Love may dream on unto eternity ⟨The soul dreams on
   thru all th'eternity⟩

 235/11 habitants] ⟨citizens⟩ *STN.*

To Ysolt. For Pardon (p. 235).
235/24 held] ⟨had⟩

For Ysolt. The Triad of Dawn (p. 236). *Before this sequence in the notebook, Pound wrote the heading, "To Follow. 'For Astarte'/The Seven of Dule." The material indicated by this heading is not in the notebook, and has not yet been discovered.*
236/11 is] ⟨hath⟩
236/11 might should] ⟨might might⟩
236/13 availeth] ⟨shall value⟩
236/20 mock'ry] ⟨mocking⟩
236/25 dammed] *STN has footnote:* dammed—within
236/28 heat] ⟨might⟩
237/8 bard] ⟨joy⟩
237/8] *Fair copy, in ink, ends here; lines 9–14 added in pencil.*
237/10 chords] ⟨charms⟩

Piazza San Marco (p. 238).
238/12] *Fair copy, in ink, ends here; poem was resumed in pencil but never finished. Following 238/14 is a draft of several more lines, apparently as follows:*

Some comfort 'tis, it gie'a mon a wondrous human feelin'
for Bobbi sinned, it might be some relief
to know just how high Mt. Parnassus fief
was gied to Herod's swines, or what squealing
pig has the right to wave[?] this word[?] "stealing"

Lotus-bloom (p. 239). *Part II, lines 14–21 (240/14–21), were published separately, with slight alteration, under the title "Xenia": see above, P, p. 82. In the manuscript these lines are followed by a penciled insertion:* (of these my rime!) *The remainder of part II (lines 1–13 and 22–30, or 240/1–13 and 240/22–30) along with the first four lines of Part IV are canceled in the manuscript, and part II has been given the title:* "Coda to Ysolt."

For the Triumph of the Arts (p. 244). *The subtitle* "Jacques Chardinel, of the Albigenses" *and the final parenthetical line appear to have been added to the poem in revision. At the same time, apparently, the following lines were canceled: II(1–6, 13–25; or 244/17–20; 245/1–2; and 245/9–21. The poem is published here without omission.*

Fragment to W. C. W.'s Romance (p. 246). *The* "Romance" *is apparently a long poem, a chivalric romance in blank verse, written by Williams about this time. Pound evidently had seen the poem in manuscript, a copy of which was also sent to Viola Scott Baxter [Jordan], and which is now preserved in the Beinecke Library.*

In That Country (p. 248). *Title, omitted from notebook text, is that assigned to poem in Pound's table of contents in STN.*
248/12 forge of thine own soul] ⟨from thine own soul to forge⟩
248/13 Thy] ⟨one⟩
248/16 some other] ⟨another⟩

Autumnus (p. 249).
   Title] *Ts. has subtitle:* (An Antistave for Ernest Dowson's "Spring of the Soul").
   Ts. is dated "Smart Set July 23," *and presumably was submitted to the magazine on that date in 1908.*

Ballad of Wine Skins (p. 251). *On a separate page following this poem, Pound has written the line:* Some great dim soul that dieth of desire, *apparently as the first line of a poem that was never included in the notebook.*

Shalott (p. 252). *Title, omitted from notebook text, is that assigned to poem in Pound's table of contents to STN.* "Shalott" *is followed in STN by a draft of an essay, as follows:*
All art begins in the physical discontent (or torture) of loneliness and partiality.
   It is ⟨was⟩ to fill this lack that man first spun shapes out of the void. And with the intensity ⟨intensifying⟩ of this longing gradually came unto him power, power over the essences of the dawn, over the filaments of light and the warp of melody.
   And I?
   Of the dawn's reflexion as you see here, feeling the flowing of the essences of beauty [here color chiefly, as I remember] until they gradually grouped themselves into form.
   Of such perceptions rise the ancient myths of the origin of demi-gods. Even as the ancient myths of metamorphosis rise out of flashes of cosmic consciousness.
   vid. The Tree. [an attempt to express a sensation or perception which revealed to me the inner matter of the Daphne story].
   Perhaps some will dispute my term "form" as used above. Perception of form is not perception of matter but of space matter does or might fill. But I will not dispute nor claim that I use the word in the ordinary sense.
   Certainly the beauty of the morning of which I write took unto itself a personality.
   Perhaps of the spirit of beauty of which I yet felt a particular "one" a signet in mortality.
   Art and marriage are not incompatible but marriage means art death often because there are so few sufficiently great to avoid the semi-stupor of satisfied passion—whence no art is.
   The essay draft in ink ends at the word incompatible *in the final paragraph. The passage following, from* but marriage means *to* whence no art is *has been added in pencil.*

For Italico Brass (p. 253).
253/9 its] ⟨her⟩
254/10 braggart] ⟨stalwart⟩ ⟨sluggard⟩

Envoi (p. 255). *The manuscript of "Envoi" shows much revision, including four canceled versions of the last two lines (255/13–14) before the final version.*

Statement of Being (p. 257). *First published: A(1958).*

Swinburne: A Critique (p. 261).
Title] In the title and last line of the poem, ts. has Swinbourne. *Pound may have intended some special archaic effect by this spelling, but at 261/8 the ts. has* Swinbuurne, *apparently a typing error. We have modernized the spelling of the name throughout.*

The Summons (p. 262). *The Pound Archive has three typescripts; we have followed for our text what appears to be the last, marked* Finale *and signed in Pound's hand.*
262/17 dew of sweet] fragrant dew of *tss. 1, 2.*
262/18 quaint] sweet *ts. 1.*
262/19 broidered] the *ts. 1.*
262/26 gay] sweet careless *tss. 1, 2.*
262/26 yester-year] ⟨yesterday⟩ *ts. 2.*
263/2 the shadow] a shadow *tss. 1, 2.*
263/3–17] *omitted ts. 1.*
263/4 as I am ever] ever as I am *ts. 2.*
263/13 Must we] Must we ever *ts. 2.*

Capilupus Sends Greetings to Grotus (p. 266). *The Pound Archive has two typescripts, the second of which (ts. 2) appears to be later and more reliable, and which we have therefore followed for our text. Unfortunately, the extant copy of ts. 2 lacks a page, and we have supplied the missing lines (236/26 through 237/16) from ts. 1.*
Title] Mantua 1500 and footnote omitted ts. 1.
266/9 thou dost] *omitted ts. 1.*
266/23 grass] grasses *ts. 1.*
266/24 to] on *ts. 1.*
267/4 manner] stile *ts. 1.*
267/20 such] they *ts. 1.*
267/26 tool to] tool wherewith to *ts. 1.*

The Hills (p. 269). *The Pound Archive has two typescripts, one of which has the manuscript notation* Munsey *(indicating possible submission to Munsey's Magazine) and the date* Apr. 27.07.

"Chommoda" (p. 272). *The typescript of "Chommoda" is typed on the* back of a sheet from a letter from John Quinn, suggesting a date of composition for the poem in early 1915, or perhaps a little later.

PAX SATURNI (p. 277). *Reprinted: Collected Shorter Poems (1968), with the title "Reflection and Advice," the original title as submitted to Poetry, but changed in correspondence. The reprinted version omits the epigraph and lines 30–35 (278/5–10).*

XENIA: I, II (p. 278). *These two poems headed a group published together under the heading "Xenia." The others, later published separately and collected in P2, were: III–V [A Song of the Degrees, I–III]; VI [Ité]; VII. Dum capitolium scandet.*

THE CHOICE (p. 279). *Reprinted: New Freewoman (1 Dec. 1913) The New Poetry (1917) L2.*
Title] The Preference *L2*.

XENIA: IV, V (p. 279). *These two poems were numbers IV and V in a group under the heading "Zenia" apparently an error for "Xenia." The others, later published separately and collected in P2, were: [I. To Dives]; II. [Alba]; III. (Epitaph); VI. [Causa]; VII. [The Bath Tub]; VIII. [Arides]; IX. [The Encounter]; X. Simulacra; XI. (Tame Cat). Reprinted: Collected Shorter Poems (1968) [V. "She had a pig-shaped face" only, with the title "The Rapture."]*
279/17 As long as her head was averted] As long as she looked away *CSP*

HOMAGE TO WILFRED SCAWEN BLUNT (p. 281). *Reprinted: Egoist (2 Feb. 1914) Poetry (Mar. 1914) Some Contemporary Poets (1920).*

OUR RESPECTFUL HOMAGES TO M. LAURENT TAILHADE (p. 283). *Reprinted: Collected Shorter Poems (1968).*
283/1 OM MANI PADME HUM] *omitted CSP.*
283/2 LET US ERECT A COLUMN, an epicene column, / To Monsieur Laurent Tailhade!] Come let us erect a phallic column to Laurent Tailhade. *CSP.*
283/7 Monsieur] *omitted CSP.*

ANOTHER MAN'S WIFE (p. 285). *Reprinted: Others anthology (1916).*

POEM: ABBREVIATED FROM THE CONVERSATION OF MR. T. E. H[ULME]. (p. 286). *Reprinted: U.*

REFLECTION (p. 286). *Unsigned in Smart Set; probably by Pound.*

TO A CITY SENDING HIM ADVERTISEMENTS (p. 287).
287/6 songs you] songs that you *ms.*
287/23 Are] ⟨No⟩ *ms.*
287/25 have fooled] have also fooled *ms.*

INDEX OF TITLES

INDEX OF FIRST LINES

328